The right of Dennis Sherwood to be identified as the author of this work has been asserted in accordance with the Copyright, Designs and Patents Act 1988

First published 2002 by
Capstone Publishing (a Wiley company)
8 Newtec Place
Magdalen Road
Oxford OX4 1RE
United Kingdom
http://www.capstoneideas.com

CIP catalogue records for this book are available from the British Library and the US Library of Congress

ISBN 1-84112-306-4

Printed and bound by CPI Antony Rowe, Eastbourne

This book is printed on acid-free paper

Substantial discounts on bulk quantities of Capstone books are available to corporations, professional associations and other organizations. Please contact Capstone for more details on +44 (0)1865 798 623 or (fax) +44 (0)1865 240 941 or (e-mail) info@wiley-capstone.co.uk

Contents

Introduction to ExpressExec

ExpressExec is 3 million words of the latest management thinking compiled into 10 modules. Each module contains 10 individual titles forming a comprehensive resource of current business practice written by leading practitioners in their field. From brand management to balanced scorecard, ExpressExec enables you to grasp the key concepts behind each subject and implement the theory immediately. Each of the 100 titles is available in print and electronic formats.

Through the ExpressExec.com Website you will discover that you can access the complete resource in a number of ways:

» printed books or e-books;
» e-content – PDF or XML (for licensed syndication) adding value to an intranet or Internet site;
» a corporate e-learning/knowledge management solution providing a cost-effective platform for developing skills and sharing knowledge within an organization;
» bespoke delivery – tailored solutions to solve your need.

Why not visit www.expressexec.com and register for free key management briefings, a monthly newsletter and interactive skills checklists. Share your ideas about ExpressExec and your thoughts about business today.

Please contact elound@wiley-capstone.co.uk for more information.

Introduction to Innovation

This chapter explains why the organizational ability to innovate – to solve problems, to discover new ways of doing things, to grasp opportunities – confers ultimate competitive advantage.

INNOVATION – THE ULTIMATE COMPETITIVE ADVANTAGE

Isn't it wonderful when your business possesses some magic "silver bullet?" Perhaps it's a blockbuster product that takes the global market by storm – like a Sony Walkman; maybe it's a fundamentally new business process – like Amazon.com – which achieves that elusive "double" of significantly reducing cost *and* improving customer service at the same time. Or maybe it's an untarnishable brand, like Virgin or Coca-Cola. Yes, these silver bullets are indeed immensely valuable.

There's just one problem. Time. Yes, a silver bullet is fantastic, but, sooner or later, time will take its toll. Even the greatest product will become obsolete, old-fashioned, redundant. I remember, before my final university exams, I bought myself a top-of-the-range slide rule, a truly world-leading product, manufactured by Faber Castell. I still have it – as a souvenir of the old times: not long afterwards, I bought my first Hewlett-Packard calculator.

Even the slickest process will no longer win the business Olympic Gold Medal of quickest, cheapest, most modern. Every process is, after all, an artefact of current technology and, as technology evolves, so processes, however good at the time they were developed, lose their leading edge.

And no brand is untarnishable. For decades, Marks & Spencer was by far the leading retail brand in the UK, as well as being a great share investment, and one of the most attractive companies to work for. But by 2001, it had *lost* more shareholder value over the preceding three years than any other company in the UK.

Silver bullets, then, are great while they last. But they cannot last for ever.

What, then, is even better than a silver bullet?

It's a machine that builds them. Again and again and again and again. Surely, if you can build within your organization a machine that can manufacture silver bullets, then whenever one is beginning to lose its magic, you can be confident that another, then another, then another and then yet another are on their way.

What does such a machine look like? What are its major components? And how can you build one?

Well, the machine looks like your organization. Not quite the way it is now, maybe, but like the way it can be made to look, if you have the will to do it, and if you have the "design specification." For its major component is the *organizational capability to innovate*, to solve problems, to have great ideas, to develop new ways of doing things – even if there isn't an explicit "problem to solve." If innovation can become your organization's "core competence," then this truly confers the ultimate competitive advantage. And how can you build one? Well, that's what this volume, and the companion ExpressExec title *Creating an Innovative Culture*, are all about ...

Definition of Terms:
What is Innovation?

This chapter defines innovation as a four-stage process of idea generation, evaluation, development and implementation.

WHAT, PRECISELY, DO WE MEAN BY INNOVATION?

''Innovation'' is one of those words that can mean different things to different people – indeed, if you ask a group of your colleagues to write a sentence or two about what they mean by the term, you should expect a lot of variety, for example:

» ''A new idea.''
» ''A really great new product.''
» ''Something different from the competition.''
» ''Something that makes real money.''
» ''Something that is so radically different, it blows the competition out of the water!''

Some people tend to emphasize the ''creativity'' aspect of innovation; others stress the need for commercial success; yet others highlight the importance of being ''radical.''

Well, all these definitions have some validity, so let's enrich them.

INNOVATION AS A PROCESS

Let's first think of innovation as a process. Certainly, the heart of innovation is the ''creative act,'' that spark of inspiration (or whatever it is) that triggers that fantastic new idea. Now, if you work in a university, for example, that could well be enough – you can think about the idea for a while, discuss it with colleagues, speak about it at conferences, write some journal articles, maybe even write a book.

But in a commercial or organizational context, having a great idea just is not enough. Something has to happen to that idea – others have to be persuaded of its relevance; perhaps money has to be spent trying it out, maybe building some models, or testing a prototype; if the new idea is a new product, then perhaps some new manufacturing plant has to be built, and there will certainly have to be some sort of marketing campaign around the product launch. Bringing a new idea to full fruition, *so that something real actually happens*, requires much more work than just having the idea in the first place.

In the commercial world, innovation is a process which starts with an idea, and results in something real actually having happened, such as the launch of a new product or the implementation of a new process, and one way of capturing this is in terms of the *Innovation Target* (Fig. 2.1):

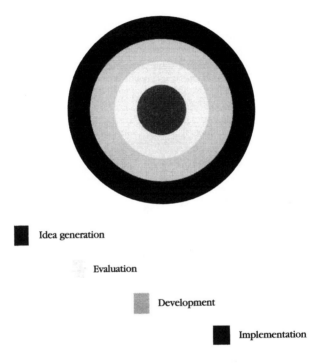

■ Idea generation

Evaluation

Development

■ Implementation

Fig. 2.1   The Innovation Target.

This diagram illustrates that innovation in business is a sequence of four stages:

1 *Idea generation* – in which the initial ideas are created.
2 *Evaluation* – in which a decision is taken as to which ideas to progress, and which to discard, at least for the present.

3 *Development* – in which an idea is made fully fit-for-purpose.
4 *Implementation* – in which the idea is brought to full fruition.

DOMAINS OF APPLICATION

Most people think of innovation in the context of a "better mouse-trap" – a new product or service that outstrips all its predecessors. Certainly, better products and services are an important application of innovation, but by no means the only one, as the following overlay to the Innovation Target (Fig. 2.2) suggests:

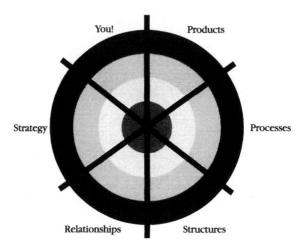

Fig. 2.2 The Innovation Target plus overlay.

The application of innovation to the creation of new products and services is shown in the top right-hand segment, but, following the diagram around, innovation also applies to:

» *processes* – as exemplified by the best examples of business process re-engineering

» *structures* – in terms of new forms of organization
» *relationships* – for example, new forms of external relationships with customers or suppliers, or new forms of internal relationships within your own organization
» *strategy* – in the form of not only new innovative strategies, but also as regards the process of strategy formulation
» *you!* – for maybe the most fundamental form of innovation is the acceptance, within my mind – or indeed your mind – that maybe there really is a better idea out there!

Innovation is the whole of this space: the four-stage process, plus the application domains. So, if you want to be better at innovation, and to manage innovation as an organizational competence, then all of these aspects need to be encompassed. Since the process stages underpin all the applications, let me describe each of these four stages more fully.

Idea generation

The center of the Innovation Target represents *idea generation*. In the absence of new ideas, there is nothing to evaluate, nothing to develop, nothing to implement, and so idea generation is truly the heart of the entire innovation process.

Idea generation is synonymous with creativity, but as soon as the word "creativity" is mentioned, most people begin to make mental associations with concepts such as "creative people," "genius," "special gift" and the like – associations driven by the popularly-held belief that creativity – the personal ability to generate new ideas – is an especially rare talent with which only the fortunate few are born.

I disagree.

I believe that it is a skill that can be learnt, and, as with all human skills, its application is enhanced with practice. I will describe the skill itself in Chapter 6, and give some examples of its application in Chapter 7.

Evaluation

Evaluation – the second zone from the centre of the Innovation Target – is the process by which ideas are selected for further develop-ment, or, alternatively, are rejected. Stated as imply as that, evaluation sounds as if it's a well-ordered and effective process that every business does in a professional way as a matter of course.

In reality, though, evaluation is a much more complex process. What happens, for example, if someone junior in your organization makes a "radical" suggestion? In all probability, the idea will very quickly be dismissed as lunatic, and the meeting will move on to more "serious" suggestions. And, as a result, the junior manager will have learnt a most important organizational lesson: to be very careful about when to open her mouth, and even more careful about what she ever dares to suggest. But that's not the only result. The organization has lost out too, for by dissuading someone from making a suggestion, the organization is losing the opportunity for someone else to build on the original suggestion, and take it further, perhaps to a very good idea indeed. As we shall see in Chapter 6, an important part of the idea generation process is the way in which teams work together, with people spring-boarding off one another's contributions – a process that can work only if individuals are willing to make a contribution in the first place.

What is happening here, of course, is the process of evaluation – but few of us think of this natural, everyday business interaction in such formal terms. An idea has been tabled – that the organization might do something radically different – and as soon as the words are uttered, we immediately form a judgment as to whether the idea is "good" or "bad." What else is this but evaluation? And how do we make this judgment? Are we influenced by who made the suggestion? Are we influenced by whether or not we are potentially threatened by the suggestion? Or by whether we immediately like or dislike the idea? Or by whether or not we like the person who suggested the idea? Or whether or not we feel it is in our career interests to be seen to be supporting the idea, opposing it, or remaining detached?

My experience is that we are influenced by all of these things, and many more too. Our reaction to new ideas – especially radical ones – is a complex mixture of detached judgment and personal emotion, of business experience and organizational politics.

But is there a way of conducting the process of idea evaluation in a more robust, professional manner? A way that encourages people to continue to suggest ideas without feeling they are risking their careers, but one that still filters out the lulus, so we don't bet the company either? A way that clearly identifies the risks associated with the idea, enabling us to determine how those risks can be assessed and managed? Clearly, what we are seeking is a question of balance: a process that stimulates idea generation, but can still distinguish the pie-in-the sky from the blockbuster; a process that avoids the worst of organizational politics, but rewards integrity and honesty; a process that passes the "due diligence" test that enables us to say with pride, even five years later, that the decision we took was the best possible, given the information we had at the time.

The good news is that such as process does indeed exist: I outline it in Chapter 10, and in more detail in the accompanying title *Creating an Innovative Culture*.

Development

Development – the third zone from the centre of the Innovation Target – is the process by which an idea is proven to be a practical reality. For some ideas, the development process might be very short, requiring only a feasibility study (many ideas for process improvement, for example); for others, however, the development process may take many years, and be very difficult. The archetypal example here is the development process for a new drug, for which the activities of pre-clinical investigation, clinical trials and the gaining of approval from the regulatory authorities can be enormously arduous, lengthy and expensive.

Indeed, as we cross the boundary between evaluation and development, something very important happens – the resources of people, time and money which are required to make the idea happen, to develop it, and subsequently implement it, are usually much, much more than resources required to generate the idea and evaluate it.

As we shall see in detail in Chapter 6, individuals can be very creative in generating great ideas, and small groups can be even more powerful; small project teams are also all that is usually required for even the most thorough evaluation. But when we come to development, and subsequent implementation, much greater resources usually need to be mobilized.

This has two consequences. First, the deployment of resources usually requires organizational co-ordination and commitment: although an individual can have a great idea, only in the most trivial cases can the individual alone bring the idea to full fruition. Second, the risk to the organization, and perhaps also to the individuals working on the project, increases: there is much more at stake if the project should fail.

The first point is about organizational style, behavior and culture, and the ease with which the organization can form, manage, and subsequently disband project teams. It is also about the skills of the organization in managing projects, and its experience and expertise in managing project uncertainties. The second point is about risk – and indeed the themes of risk and risk management underpin much about innovation.

Innovation is fundamentally about risk. Innovation, by definition, is doing something you have not done before. And, as a consequence, this must entail risk. The unwillingness of some organizations, or some people, to take all but the safest risks is one of the reasons why those organizations, and those people, shy away from innovation. In today's business climate, however, there is a strong argument that the perceived low-risk option of maintaining the *status quo*, or of following others, is in fact more risky than stepping into the unknown by innovating!

Wise organizations, and good managers, however, are not daunted by the existence of risk: rather, they are much more concerned about the mechanisms and processes by which the risks inevitably associated with innovation can be:

» *identified*, so we know what and where they are;
» *understood*, so we know how they are likely to arise, and the impact each is likely to have should any in fact crystallize;
» *monitored*, so we can have as early warning as possible of the likely occurrence of the risk;
» *managed*, so we know how to reduce the likelihood of the risk, and what we need to do should the risk in fact come to pass.

And – more significantly – they do not wait until one of the risks hits to identify, understand, monitor, and manage it: they have done this in advance. When?

During evaluation.

One of the most important functions – if not *the* single most important function – of the evaluation process is to understand the risks of the innovation project, and to define how those risks are to be managed. These are all strongly dependent on an organization's culture, a theme I explore in detail in the accompanying title *Creating an Innovative Culture*; what we need to note here is that the organization should not even contemplate embarking on development unless it has the appetite, conviction, and resources to see the project right through both the development and implementation stages – a commitment made while anticipating all the risks.

The evaluation zone therefore acts as a filter – the exercise of business wisdom in selecting those ideas which bring sufficient business benefit, even in the light of the well-researched risks, from those that do not.

Implementation

The outermost zone of the Innovation Target – representing implementation – concerns all those activities that take a proven idea into full fruition. For ideas concerning process improvement, today this usually involves the building of a new IT system; for a new product, this can involve new factory facilities, an enhanced supply chain, training of sales and support staff, as well as all the marketing activities heralding the launch. There is clearly a lot to be done.

Certainly, all the remarks already made concerning organizational co-ordination, the demand on organizational resources, and managing risk, apply even more to implementation than they do to development, and from the point of view of "making innovation happen," development and implementation dovetail smoothly into one another.

There are, however, two particular aspects of implementation which are unique to this stage, and merit attention: criteria of success, and learning.

Every new idea carries high hopes, especially in the mind of the idea's originator. But when an idea receives the full organizational backing required for development and implementation, these hopes are often magnified and augmented until they become not only expectations, but the performance measures by which the idea, the development and implementation project, and – much more importantly – the individual members of the project team, are judged as successes – or failures.

What are the criteria by which the implementation is to be regarded as a success, or indeed a failure? What are the performance measures? Where do they come from? What is their validity? Given that innovation is all about moving into uncharted territory, how do you know when you've got there?

Which performance measures should be applied to implementation? And how do the performance measures applied to implementation relate to the commitments implied way back when the idea was evaluated?

This discussion of performance measures leads naturally to the topic of learning. However thorough the development process, it isn't until the idea is fully implemented that you can assess the extent to which the idea truly works in practice. You should not be surprised if the outcome is different from what you expected; wise managers seek to learn new things from each new experience, rather than forcing their previous learning on to a new world.

SUMMARY

The key message of this chapter is that the term "innovation" refers to all the four stages of:

» idea generation
» evaluation
» development, and
» implementation

as applied to:

» new product development
» new process development
» organizational innovation
» relationship innovation
» strategic innovation, and
» you!

Managing these is complex and difficult, but it can be done! This title, and the accompanying title, *Creating an Innovative Culture*, will give you great insights into the tools and techniques of deliberate and systematic idea generation, and into the cultural requirements for success overall, but especially in evaluation, development, and implementation. As a starting point, you might like to ask these questions of your organization . . .

HOW GOOD IS YOUR ORGANIZATION AT INNOVATION?

Here are some questions that will help throw some initial light on how good your organization is at innovation.

» What new ideas have successfully been implemented by your organization in the last three years?
» Who originated those ideas?
» What was the nature of the process by which those ideas were evaluated?
» What were the plans and budgets originally agreed for the development and implementation of each idea?
» How did the actual outcome of the development and implementation compare to the original plans and budgets?
» What were the originally targeted performance measures for success?
» What happened to the members of successful project teams?
» What happened to members of projects that were regarded as failures?
» What was learned from the successes?
» And what from the failures?
» How has that learning been captured, internalized, communicated, and used?

Evolution of Innovation

This chapter describes the contributions to innovation made by people such as Isaac Newton, Thomas Edison, Alex Osborne, Edward de Bono and Arthur Koestler.

THE SEARCH FOR NEW IDEAS IS AS OLD AS TIME

Man's spirit of curiosity, of seeking better ways of doing things, of invention, has been an integral aspect of the human condition ever since the emergence of man as a distinct species around two million years ago.

Originally, before the invention of agriculture (one of the most profound innovations man has ever achieved), the early humans were hunter-gatherers, finding their food by hunting animals, fish and birds, and gathering vegetable products from their natural habitats. Biologically, one of the key factors ensuring survival was the development of memory – memory of where to find the right plants to eat, or where to find the best places to hunt. The evolution of the human brain facilitated the enrichment of memory, and the enrichment of memory stimulated the brain. Throughout this process, man's ability to break away from pre-conditioned behaviors was enhanced, as was his ability to discover new things, to have new ideas, to innovate.

It has also been known for a very long time that having new ideas can be dangerous too. Many inventors have been regarded as at least partially mad, if not wholly so, and even today, innovation is often associated with wackiness, and the rejection of the normal codes of behavior. By definition, innovation is about something new, and when that something new is a challenge to the existing order, those in authority, or those who have a vested interest in preserving the *status quo*, can react very harshly – and powerfully – indeed. Galileo famously stood trial to defend his assertion that the earth moved around the sun – and lost – even though this was not a new idea at all, but can be traced back to the ancient Greek philosopher Aristarchus of Samos; and more than a century before Galileo's trial, Niccolo Macchiavelli wrote a telling paragraph in *The Prince*. The original language of *The Prince* is renaissance Florentine Italian, and there are a number of slightly different translations, of which this is one:

"The innovator makes enemies of all those who prospered under the old order . . . and whenever those who oppose the changes can do so, they attack vigorously."

Those words were written around 1514, yet they still ring true to anyone who has dared to suggest an idea different from the big boss's.

From Newton to de Bono

Despite the political – and sometimes personal – difficulties in making innovation actually happen, inventions continued (thank heaven!) to be made, and innovators refused to give up. And throughout this time, there has always been one fundamental question: is creative talent an inborn, innate ability which only the fortunate few possess?

To those who are naturally "creative," there is often a strong incentive to answer this question with a very assertive "yes" – if I possess a talent that you don't, then this confers power, influence and exclusivity. And over time, people – particularly those whose self-perception is that they are "uncreative" ("if I was creative, I'd be a pop star, not an accountant, wouldn't I?") – begin to believe the same thing.

There are, however, many clues that perhaps things aren't so black and white. One of the greatest creative geniuses of all time, Sir Isaac Newton, the scientist who codified gravity and did much fundamental research in mechanics, optics, and physics, as well as in mathematics, wrote in 1675, "If I have seen further it is by standing on the shoulders of giants," thus acknowledging that his ideas were based solidly on the foundations of the ideas of his predecessors. Thomas Alva Edison, probably the single most inventive man who has ever lived (Edison held 1,093 patents, and his inventions include the electric filament light bulb and the phonograph – the predecessor of the gramophone and the CD player), said in an article published in a 1932 issue of *Life* magazine, "invention is one percent inspiration and ninety-nine perspiration" – emphasizing the importance of sheer hard work in the innovation process.

But perhaps the greatest spur to making innovation, and especially its heartland idea generation, into a systematic process came not from universities or the R&D function of big business but from advertising. The increasing use of advertising in the years between the two World Wars last century made innovation – in the guise of advertising slogans – a highly profitable activity, and it made good commercial sense to be deliberately good at it.

Alex Osborne was one of the founders of the famous Madison Avenue advertising agency BBD&O (the O stands for Osborne). He became increasingly interested in how to make idea generation a deliberate, systematic process, and he was acutely aware of the Machiavelli problem – that if the environment in which idea generation is to take place is in any sense unsafe, then it just won't happen. He therefore designed a process, to take place in a specifically "safe" environment, to help make ideas happen – a process which, in 1939, he termed "brainstorming" – a process used worldwide to this day. Osborne also founded a centre for research into the innovative process, The Centre for Studies in Creativity at Buffalo State College, one of the University Colleges within the State University of New York.

But perhaps the most well-known method of creating new ideas is "lateral thinking" – a term coined by Edward de Bono in his book *Lateral Thinking for Management*, first published in 1967. De Bono distinguished between "vertical thinking," which follows a specific chain of logical deduction so that a premise leads remorselessly to a conclusion, and "lateral thinking," a process of idea generation which he – to my mind correctly – argued was necessarily different. Logic is designed to drive you from A to B; for example, as in proving all those geometrical theorems you did long ago at school. Although it is possible that arrival at B might be new to you, it is most likely that someone else (such as your geometry teacher) has been there before, and so de Bono argued that pure logic is primarily a process to take you down paths others have previously discovered. But if the purpose of innovation in general and idea generation in particular is to find new paths, then following previously determined paths of logic is unlikely to do this particularly well. To discover new paths, de Bono reasoned, we must use a different thinking process – lateral thinking.

It is at this point that many people have difficulty, for there is an immediate reaction against moving away from the power of logic. This reaction is driven by the assumption that anything that is not logical must, by definition, be illogical. And things that are illogical must be odd, nuts, crazy, mad. So, if something is perceived to be illogical, it is rejected immediately.

Well, consider the possibility that there are not just two states of reasoning – the logical and the illogical. What if there were a third state which we might call non-logical? Non-logical thinking is neither logical nor illogical, just different: a way of thinking that follows neither the step-by-step audit trail of logic, nor the random ravings of the madhouse. A way that is intuitive and inspirational, and which can be rationalized with hindsight rather than foresight. Just as that which is not-black is not necessarily white – it might be blue or green – then that which is not logical need not be illogical, it might be non-logical, different. And if we can learn the "rules" of this very different game, then maybe we can learn to be more creative.

Since 1967, de Bono has spent his entire career evangelizing about lateral thinking, and, as I write this in the early summer of 2001, he continues unabated; he has also been markedly successful – as he never tires of pointing out, the term "lateral thinking" is now to be found in the Oxford English Dictionary and so is officially part of the English language, and almost everyone you might meet has heard of the term, knowing – loosely – what it means. This does not mean, however, that many people actually know how to do it . . .

But Koestler got there first

Arthur Koestler was born in Hungary in 1905, and died – by his own hand – in London in 1983. In the intervening 78 years, he led a most remarkable life, combining the worlds of the man of letters with the man of action, of the intellectual esthete with the passionate lover. He was nominated three times for the Nobel Prize, and served in the French Foreign Legion during the Second World War. As a journalist covering the Spanish Civil War, he was captured by Franco's troops and sentenced to death, surviving only as a result of the intervention of the British Government. This provided him with the raw material for one of the most chilling books I have ever read, *Darkness at Noon*, which transfers Koestler's experience in Spain to a condemned cell in Stalin's Russia.

And he also found time to articulate what to me is the most profound description of creativity that I have ever read – a definition I now refer to as Koestler's Law:

"The creative act is not an act of creation in the sense of the Old Testament."

"It does not create something out of nothing; it uncovers, selects, reshuffles, combines, synthesizes already existing facts, ideas, faculties, skills."

"The more familiar the parts, the more striking the new whole."

This is a quotation from Koestler's book *The Act of Creation*, published in 1964. This book is a (highly academic) enquiry into the nature of creativity, in which Koestler explores creativity in art, in drama, in literature, in intellectual endeavor. His conclusion is that the nature of creativity in all these fields is identical – it is a process of forming new patterns from pre-existing components. What is different is the emotional engagement – or indeed disengagement. In drama and literature, for example, much of the creative skill of the author is in drawing the theater-goer's or reader's emotions ever more strongly into the play or the story. And if you have ever wiped a tear from your eye in a theater or a cinema, or rejoiced with elation as the heroine lives happily ever after, then you know just how powerful this can be.

Humor, on the other hand, is emotionally detached: you are on the outside looking in. When the pompous man slips on the banana skin, we all laugh at how his false dignity merits its just reward. But we also know that the fall can hurt.

Intellectual creativity is emotionally neutral – we are neither engaged nor disengaged; we are solving an abstract problem.

To me, Koestler's Law is a statement of great insight, and we shall explore this in depth in Chapter 6. Before leaving *The Act of Creation*, however, let me just note that much of the book is also about the process of idea generation itself, a process Koestler calls "thinking aside."

THE CURRENT STATE OF THE ART

Today, innovation is very much on the corporate agenda. At the dizzy heights of strategy, Gary Hamel's latest book *Leading the Revolution* is a polemic in favor of "business concept innovation" – the total rethinking of a organization's entire business model – written with a passion, energy and zeal of which arch-revolutionary Karl Marx himself would be proud. And at the more prosaic level of "yes, you too can have great new ideas," there are any number of books describing tools and techniques which you can use to help you generate new ideas. Ros Jay's *The Ultimate Book of Business Creativity* lists 36, neatly in alphabetical order, from "The 7 × 7 Technique" to "Verbal Checklist;" *101 Ways to Generate Great Ideas* by Timothy Foster claims 101; and *Techniques of Structured Problem Solving* by Arthur VanGundy catalogues no fewer than 250!

I must declare a vested interest here, for I too have contributed to the clutter on the bookshelves. In *Smart Things to Know about Innovation and Creativity* I argue the case that, despite the fact that VanGundy does indeed identify 250 different named techniques, they largely fall into two families – families that I call "springboards" and "retro-fits." I shall explain all in Chapter 6, but let me now turn to an important aspect of business life today, e-novation.

The E-Dimension

This chapter argues that although technology is both a spur to and facilitator of innovation, there is much scope for innovation way beyond technology's boundaries.

INNOVATION IS MORE THAN E-NOVATION

The e-boom was a major spurt of global innovative activity, as many companies – most of them ones nobody had ever heard of – launched new businesses, new services, and often new business models too. At the height of the boom, it looked as if innovation was dead, and that the only scope for doing new things was by e-novation.

As the boom turned to bust, public sentiment turned the other way. The share prices of the technology sector plummeted, venture capitalists hardened their investment criteria, and budding entrepreneurs abandoned (no doubt reluctantly) their hopes of palaces and executive jets, and returned to their garages and motorbikes.

No doubt, as time passes, things will become more balanced, with e-businesses and e-opportunities taking their legitimate place alongside other "more conventional" forms of business activity. There is no doubt, however, that the explosion of technological opportunity will have a major long-term impact, for reasons I shall come to in a moment. But let's not forget that there is, and will continue to be, scope for conventional innovation in everything we do. If you refer back to the second target diagram for a moment (see page 8), you will see that the opportunities for innovation as regards products, processes, organization, structures, relationships, and strategy – and indeed in your own mind too – will always be present, and will transcend any particular technology-of-the-day. What makes e-novation special, however, is that it has the potential to affect all of these simultaneously, for the ease of passing messages around the Internet creates the opportunity of causing highly disruptive change, simultaneously, in many different aspects of business activity.

E-messaging has been around for a long time . . .

The ability to pass messages from one computer to another has, of course, been around for at least three decades. But to make this happen, you have to solve two major problems. First, the machines at each end have to be compatible: it's no use being able to send a message that the recipient can't understand. One solution to this is to have the same type of computer, and the associated software, at each end, which is easily done if both ends are within the same organization, but more difficult if the messages cross organizational boundaries. In this case, the only solution was to agree, amongst all the different organizations party to the message, a set of standards for how messages should be structured. The definition and agreement of such cross-industry standards is time-consuming, but by no means impossible, just one important example being the standards agreed in the UK to allow banks to transfer funds electronically through the CHAPS system, which has been in operation since 1984.

The second problem concerns the knowledge the sender of a message required about the receiver. In the past, if I wanted to send a message to a specific recipient, I needed to know the recipient's telephone number. That's fine if I know the name of the person I want to send a message to, and if I can find their telephone number, but not so good if I don't know the person's name, and even less helpful if I know their name, but can't discover the right number. The only assistance I might have had is "directory enquiries" if I knew the name but not the number, or the "Yellow Pages" if I had some idea of the nature of the organization I wanted to contact. But these are limited in their nature, and also their geography – at home I have only my local directories.

... But has been revolutionized in the last few years

E-business – if defined as the ability of organizations to transfer computer messages over long distances – has therefore been around for a long time. But what has happened in the last five years has changed the scene dramatically.

First, the problem of compatibility has largely been solved. The use of infrastructure standards such as HTML (HyperText Markup Language), the widespread adoption of the programming language JAVA, and the dominance of Microsoft, have together enabled messages written on the laptop computer I am using now to be read by almost any other computer in the world – without the need for all the computers to be from the same manufacturer, and without the need for me to agree, bilaterally, a set of standards with anyone else.

Second, the availability of web browsers and search engines has solved the problem of the requirement for prior knowledge of telephone numbers. On my laptop, I have one telephone number that connects me to the Internet. Once connected, I then have access to all the other computers in the world that are also connected, and I can find them, and communicate with them, using web browsers and search engines. These act as very sophisticated forms of "directory enquiries" and "Yellow Pages," but with the significant benefits that I no longer need to know a specific name, nor am I restricted to a short description such as "car tire retailers," nor am I limited geographically: my web browsers and search engines allow me to use a huge range of keywords and descriptive phrases to search computers all over the world. In seconds, I can discover the computer I want to connect to, no matter where it is, then make the connection directly, and so send and receive the messages I want.

And in addition, the number of people to whom I might wish to send messages to, or receive messages from, is vast. In the 1970s, when the major businesses were developing their own internal networks, the only places where you found computers were in other businesses. No one had computers at home, and laptops had not been invented. Today, the number of computers in private ownership, used primarily from the home, is huge. And the need for a stand-alone computer is diminishing fast, as televisions and mobile phones increasingly become able to provide direct Internet access.

INTERCONNECTIVITY – THE HEART OF THE E-REVOLUTION

The interconnectivity of an enormous, and growing, number of computers, combined with the increasing ease of finding what you need, stimulated by the decreasing cost of the equipment and the communications, together form the basis of the e-revolution.

At one level, e-business is an opportunity for process innovation: instead of doing my purchasing by face-to-face contact, negotiation, ordering, and invoice payment, I can streamline the process using electronic messaging. This applies as much to businesses (the business-to-business (B2B) world is driven by purchasing process innovation, particularly as regards B2B public or private purchasing exchanges) as it does to the personal shopper (as delivered by suppliers such as Amazon.com).

At another level, e-business offers much more scope for product or service innovation. If you are looking for a cheap airline ticket, for example, there are now many websites that draw together the prices of all the airlines that fly between the two cities you are looking for, and offer you a direct price comparison on a single screen. In the past, the only way you would have been able to do this was either to contact each airline one by one – a tedious thing to do – or by reference to an agent whom you trust. Now this service is available instantaneously, at any time of the day or night.

But it doesn't stop there. E-business is driving organizational innovation too, in at least two ways. Within established organizations, paper-shuffling functions and departments are now no longer needed; and within the new dot.com companies, there are all sorts of organizational innovations being explored – flatter, non-hierarchical structures, more flexible working regimes, different forms of remuneration.

But perhaps the biggest impact concerns relationship innovation. Relationship innovation concerns changes in internal relationships independent of the formal, official organization structure, and in external relationships. The fact that I can easily discover which airline offers the cheapest tickets profoundly changes my relationship with my "favorite" airline. In the past, I might have contacted that airline as my first choice, simply because I was in a hurry, and hadn't the time (or, more likely, just couldn't be bothered) to shop around. But if shopping around is much easier for me to do, then I'll do it. So much for customer loyalty. This provides a greater incentive for my favorite airline to try even harder to keep me happy, so I'll continue to buy their tickets even if they're not the cheapest. The Internet has provided – and will continue to provide – consumers with an increasing amount of relevant information, and so gives consumers, both as a group and individually, huge power.

Another key relationship which is in the process of changing is that between an organization and its key stakeholders, such as shareholders or a wider public. Only a few years ago, listed companies produced a glossy annual report, and perhaps a few flimsy interim reports during the year. Many annual reports are now published on the Internet, thus creating pressure for more information, more often. How long will it be before companies begin to publish their management accounts, or even their budgets?

WHY E-NOVATION IS ESPECIALLY IMPORTANT RIGHT NOW

The umbrella concept of e-business therefore straddles product innovation, process innovation, organizational innovation, and relationship innovation – and as a consequence, strategic innovation too, for the existence of the Internet must influence the strategy of all organizations. The e-world encompasses the whole of the Innovation Target, and that's why it is especially significant right now.

The Global Dimension

This chapter asserts that innovation knows no boundaries, and addresses the key question of how to make your organization more innovative.

INNOVATION KNOWS NO BOUNDARIES

Innovation is a fundamental human activity. We are all curious, we all want to discover and learn new things. There are no intrinsic constraints on innovation attributable to geography; nor, from a historic perspective, is there any indication that one part of the globe has been inherently more innovative than any other. For sure, some countries have produced more innovations and inventions at different times in history – China in ancient times, the Arab world during the European "dark ages," the United States most recently, to name just three – but these differences are not a manifestation of differences in the fundamental human spirit. Instead, they reflect differences in the opportunity for this spirit to be set free: differences attributable to economic prosperity, and political and religious culture.

And there is a lesson for business here too. On both a local and a global scale, you can help create the financial and cultural conditions which can make innovation flourish. Or to make it die. The choice is yours.

This is a big topic, and the accompanying title in the Express-Exec series, *Creating an Innovative Culture*, examines these cultural matters in much more depth. It is appropriate, however, to mention some of the most important topics here.

HOW CAN YOU MAKE YOUR ORGANIZATION MORE INNOVATIVE?

There has been much research into how organizations can become more innovative: *The 3M Way to Innovation*, by Ernest Gundling, for example, is a study of arguably the most innovative organization in the world – a company so innovative that it has as an overall performance measure that 30% of the sales revenue in any one year must be attributable to products that were not in the catalogue four years before; James Christiansen spent three years researching this issue, publishing his findings in two highly informative books, *Competitive Innovation Management* and *Building the Innovative Organization*.

The overall conclusion of all of these studies is important:

Innovative organizations do not differ from their uninnovative competitors by virtue of having some magic, special, vital ingredient. Rather, innovative organizations deliberately manage the conventional ingredients in a special way.

One's first thought is that truly innovative organizations possess some magic factor "X" that ordinary organizations just don't have. Because they have it, they are innovative; because others don't, they aren't; if only I could discover what "X" is, and get hold of some, then my organization can be innovative too, and my problem is solved.

Unfortunately, I must inform you that a search for "X" will be as productive as the search for the elixir of youth, or the secret of transmuting base metals into gold. "X" just isn't there.

What distinguishes an innovative organization from an uninnovative one is not the presence, or absence, of some magic ingredient "X," but the way in which all the usual ingredients of normal, everyday life are managed. Let me give you an example.

As the Innovation Target shows, once an idea has passed the hurdle of evaluation, it usually then needs to be developed. Often, this requires a project team to be brought together, for a period of perhaps just a week or two, or for many months.

In an uninnovative organization, this is a struggle. People are reluctant to join a "special project" because they fear that they will lose the patronage of their line boss for appearing to be "disloyal"; or perhaps because they are anxious that their line job will no longer be available when the project is over; or perhaps because being assigned to a "special project" is perceived as a sign of imminent departure from the organization. Likewise, the boss of the person invited to join the project team may be reluctant to let the person go because it means he will have to hire a replacement, and he may think, "Why should I be the training ground for all these people disappearing on projects? What do I get out of it?" As a consequence of all this, the project is staffed by all the company rejects, all the people whose bosses are glad to see go, all the organizational no-hopers. And as a result of this, the project fails, the idea is killed, everyone says that innovation is a waste of time, and no-one, but no-one, volunteers for the next project.

Things are different in an innovative organization. Time spent on innovation development projects is recognized and rewarded, and an important criterion of promotion. The best people therefore compete for every opportunity that arises. Likewise, one aspect of the boss's role is to encourage innovation in others, and one of the boss's performance measures is all about letting staff go on projects. So, to help make this happen, the organization has procedures in place to ensure that people are mobile, and that, when one person joins a project, someone else can easily be moved in to cover the day job. Similarly, when the project is over, the original day job is not blocked, but potentially available.

Both organizations have performance measures, promotion criteria, and career development plans. The difference between the two organizations is not that one has something that the other doesn't; rather, the difference is that the innovative organization *manages* all of these coherently to support innovation, while the other doesn't.

And there is one particular aspect of organizational life that an innovative culture manages especially well, sometimes on a global scale. I call it the *BBC* . . .

THE POWER OF THE *BBC*

No, I'm not referring to the British Broadcasting Corporation – my use of these familiar initials refers, in this case, to a rather different concept: *Brain Bank Connectivity*.

Have you ever had the experience that, during a conversation or a meeting, someone else says or does something that causes you to have an idea? You don't know how it happened, or why it happened. It just happened. But you do know that it wouldn't have happened had you not been in the company of the other person.

FLOCKING

In his wonderful book *The Living Company*, Arie de Geus tells a story of two colonies of birds – robins and blue tits.

The context concerns an element of British domestic life that requires some explanation. For many decades, British households have had fresh milk delivered to their homes every day: early in the morning, the "milkman" is as regular a visitor to the house as the mailman. Usually, the milk is left by one of the doors of the house, until such time as the occupants wake up! For many years, the milk was delivered in glass bottles, sealed with an aluminum foil cap. And, just beneath the cap, if the milk is full-cream milk rather than skimmed or semi-skimmed, there is a layer of cream.

Britain is also home to many birds, including the robin and the blue tit. And, if you observe blue tits, you will see that many of them, early in the morning, after the milk has arrived but before the house occupant has awoken, will fly to the milk bottles, peck through the aluminum foil cover with their beaks, and enjoy a meal of luscious cream.

But you hardly ever see a robin do this. Why not?

It cannot be because the blue tit has evolved biologically to peck through milk-bottle tops, and the robin hasn't: the arrival of the bottles with the aluminum foil tops is far too recent to have an evolutionary explanation. Rather, the explanation is behavioral. Robins are solitary birds, who vigorously protect their own territory. Blue tits, by contrast, are gregarious and social. They share and communicate. So, when one blue tit discovered the secret of how to get some nice cream every day, he didn't keep it to himself. He told others. And the others listened – and benefited.

In Chapter 6, we'll see how innovation can be made deliberate and systematic; and how the interaction of one person with another is a major factor in the creative process. This interaction is the heart of the *BBC* – an explicit recognition that the connectivity between people enhances the creative process.

To demonstrate the power of the *BBC*, let's assume that an individual brain has a creative power of one "*creaton*" – that's a unit of measure of creativity I have just invented! Two brains, operating individually, therefore have a total creative power of two *creatons*. But if the two brains are connected, if the two people are communicating meaning-fully and co-operatively, then there is an additional contribution to their collective creativity attributable to the linkage between the brains. The total creative power of the two linked brains – the *BBC* – is therefore two *creatons* (for each of the two brains individually), plus (let's say) a further one *creaton* for the linkage: that's a total of three *creatons*. This suggests that two people working together have the potential creative power of three people working alone, for it is this additional *creaton* which captures that magic effect when a new idea is sparked as a result of the inter-personal interaction.

Now consider what happens with three connected brains, A, B and C. There are three individual brains, but there are now *four* different linkages (A and B, A and C, B and C, and the threesome A and B and C). The total *BBC* is now seven *creatons*. Something very interesting is happening, for *the number of linkages between the brains is getting bigger faster than the number of individual brains themselves.*

In fact, for a total of *n* brains, assuming that each separate link has a creative power equal to that of an individual brain, and that all linkages are of equal strength, there is a formula for the *BBC*:

For *n* linked brains, the $BBC = 2^n - 1$

So, for two brains, $n = 2$, the $BBC = 2^2 - 1$, namely, 3; likewise, for 3 brains, $n = 3$, the $BBC = 2^3 - 1$, namely, 7. And for a group of 8 brains, the *BBC* is 255! This number is vastly greater than just 8, the *BBC* of the same eight people working by themselves, individually.

I'm sure we could debate for a long time whether or not the linkage between two brains has a creative power equal to that of an individual brain, or whether all linkages are of equal strength. Well, I don't mind about that. If the power of the linkage is a different number, or if not all linkages are of equal strength, then that merely alters the arithmetic to an equation of the type:

$$BBC = n + \alpha[2^n - (n + 1)]$$

in which α is some fudge factor which expresses the creative power of a link relative to that of an individual brain.

The main point is this. The term 2^n increases very fast with *n*, and very quickly dominates the equation for the *BBC*, even for relatively small (positive and non-zero) values of the fudge factor α. That means that the creative power of a group is potentially vastly greater than that of the same number of individuals: but only if the brains are connected; only if people are talking and, more importantly, listening.

Harnessing the power of the *BBC* is, to my mind, *the* major opportunity, and *the* major challenge, for any knowledge-based industry.

In practice, of course, it doesn't necessarily have to work that way. If the fudge factor α is a negative number, then the *BBC* gets *smaller* as the number of brains increases. This happens when people become disconnected, when connections that used to exist get broken, and when brains that used to be active in creating and building the business get sidetracked. Next time you experience a "merger," you'll probably see this taking place before your very eyes.

BUT HOW DO YOU ENHANCE THE *BBC*?

The concept of the *BBC* shows convincingly that the creative power of a group is potentially much greater than that of the equivalent number of people operating by themselves – yes, the whole can be manifestly greater than the sum of the parts.

Innovative organizations know this, and make it happen. How? Easy – by ensuring that people communicate. Specifically:

They take great trouble to ensure people know one another.

You can't communicate with someone you don't know. And just because you know someone doesn't mean that you can communicate with them, because you may not like them, respect them or trust them. But just knowing them is a very good place to start.

Pick up your organization's internal telephone directory (or, these days, bring it up on your screen!). Look through it, and count the number of people you know well enough to be able to have a comfortable face-to-face conversation with. And count the number of people that you can't. Which number is bigger?

Innovative organizations ensure that as many people as possible know one another, and they do this in a very straightforward way: through training courses, in which people from different territories and business units are deliberately brought together; by ensuring that conferences and away-days are not too parochial; by seconding staff from one business unit to another. And, most importantly, they allocate budgets to make this happen. Budgets for events, budgets for travel, budgets for accommodation. That doesn't necessarily mean that everyone flies first class and stays in five-star luxury: what it does mean is that it is recognized that, to be innovative, people must meet, and that this requires sensible expenditure.

Mean organizations who scrimp on these items create barriers to stop people communicating, and they get what they deserve.

And so to me, the most important aspect of the global dimension to innovation is the scope it offers to create an incredibly powerful global brain bank. But this will happen only if the potential power of the *BBC* is indeed realized.

The State of the Art

This chapter presents ***InnovAction!***, a great process for making idea generation deliberate, systematic, transferable, repeatable and safe.

WHAT DOES KOESTLER'S LAW ACTUALLY MEAN?

I introduced Koestler's Law in Chapter 3:

> "The creative act is not an act of creation in the sense of the Old Testament.
>
> "It does not create something out of nothing; it uncovers, selects, re-shuffles, combines, synthesizes already existing facts, ideas, faculties, skills.
>
> "The more familiar the parts, the more striking the new whole."

To me, this is the most complete, and insightful, definition of creativity that I know. But what does it actually mean? And how does it apply to a business and organizational context? That's what this chapter is all about.

Koestler's Law starts by debunking a myth. Many people believe that creativity, the ability to generate stunning new ideas, is an innate gift with which only the lucky few are born. As for the rest of us, well, we needn't bother. This belief is false. Creativity is a skill that we can all learn, it is an ability we can all develop. For sure, as with all human capabilities, some people will be more talented at it than others; some people may enjoy it more than others. But no one is debarred from participating in the activity. That's what the first sentence in Koestler's Law is all about: by stating that "The creative act is not an act of creation in the sense of the Old Testament," Koestler is debunking a myth, and – at the same time – making a great statement of human empowerment.

The second part of Koestler's Law is somewhat more obscure, and rather more startling – in fact, at first sight, some people consider it to be quite wrong: surely the whole essence of creativity is that it creates something out of nothing. Isn't that what it's all about?

Well, no it isn't. Koestler is quite right.

BEETHOVEN, THE BEATLES, LITERATURE AND LIFE

To verify that Koestler is indeed right, let's spend a moment examining what some creative geniuses actually did.

Take Beethoven, for example, a true creative genius if ever there was one. But what did he actually do? Composed great symphonies, yes:

great musical works of art, yes too. But what, precisely, was the nature of his art? Well, he used music as a profound medium of expression, but not just any old music – he used music in what we recognize as the Western classical tradition. His music is not – by any means – an arbitrary jangle of random noises: on the contrary, Beethoven's music was written in the context of a well-established musical "language."

All his music, for example, was written within the framework of major and minor scales, those doh-ray-me runs of notes that children practice when they learn to play the piano. And, more fundamentally, the notes which comprise all of Beethoven's works are drawn from the same set of notes used by Bach – and the Beatles – and any other musician composing Western-style music. In fact, given a piano – which acts as a repository of all those notes – it is quite possible to play a tune that you would instantly recognize as Beethoven, the Beatles, or whoever.

So one thing that Beethoven, the Beatles, and any other composer for that matter, did *not* do was to invent any new notes.

So if Beethoven didn't invent any new notes, what *did* he do?

Given that Beethoven didn't invent any new notes, a moment's reflection will convince you that what Beethoven did was to invent very many, wonderful, emotionally powerful *patterns* of notes. The essence of Beethoven's creative genius was in taking some basic elements that already existed – the notes that you can find on a piano or any other musical instrument – and combining them simultaneously in time, and sequentially over time, into a host of astonishing patterns: patterns of rhythm, patterns of melody, patterns of harmony, patterns of dynamic intensity; patterns that we give names to, such as "Beethoven's *Fifth Symphony*," "the *Moonlight Sonata*," and " *The Ode to Joy*".

John Lennon and Paul McCartney, some 150 years later, did essentially the same thing – they took the same basic elements, the notes, and combined them into another set of new patterns, with names such as "*She Loves You*" and "*Penny Lane*". The notes are the same as Beethoven's – it's the patterns that are different.

In music, then, the creative act is well focused: it is the discovery of a new pattern of elements – the notes – that already exist. What is truly amazing about this is that the number of different elements from which all Western music is formed is incredibly small: a standard piano has only 88 different notes, and of these, only 48 are in frequent use – the very high and very low notes (the ones out of the range of the human voice) are hardly used at all. And more fundamentally still, these 48 are in fact 4 related groups of 12, these being the tones and semitones in a single octave, as represented by the repeated groups of the 7 white and 5 black notes on a piano keyboard. Just twelve fundamental elements therefore combine and recombine in a myriad of different patterns, creating the diversity of Beethoven and the Beatles, Bach and Bacharach, Handel and Holly.

This is exactly what Koestler's Law states. Musical composition "does not create something out of nothing"; rather, it "selects, re-shuffles, combines, synthesizes already existing facts . . .," where, in this case, the "facts" in question are the basic musical notes.

Music, then, is a powerful example of Koestler's Law in action. But is it a special case?

No. It isn't. Literature is very similar. All literature, whether in the form of novels, plays, or poetry, represents different patterns of pre-existing components – components we call words. Certainly, some particularly talented authors invent new words from time to time, and we delight in their invention. But inventing new words is by no means a necessary condition for creating great literature – plenty of the greatest works are comprised of words that everyone else uses, and indeed have used for centuries. And even if the author wishes to invent a new word, the process for this is exactly the same, but at the level of the word rather than the novel: to invent a new word, all you need do is discover a new pattern of pre-existing components, components which in this case are the letters (or syllables) of the appropriate language.

But an even more striking example of Koestler's Law in action is life itself. Every human being is a unique, distinct creation. And, as molecular biologists have now verified, the fundamental difference between any two human beings (and between human beings and all other living species) is attributable to the structure of the genes found in our chromosomes. The genes themselves are composed of four chemicals – adenine (A), cytosine (C), guanine (G) and thymine (T) – strung together in chains literally billions of chemicals long. With only four components, the number of different possible sequences . . . ACGTGACCTA . . . is incredibly vast. Many of these sequences are, from a biological point of view, totally meaningless, but a sufficiently large number of valid sequences exist to account for the differences between me and a sequoia tree, or between me and you. In a very true sense indeed, all biological diversity is attributable to different patterns of existing components.

BUT WHAT DOES KOESTLER'S LAW MEAN FOR BUSINESS?

As a statement of empowerment, Koestler's Law is immensely valuable. Just imagine how vibrant your business could be if all that latent creative talent, bottled up in your mind and your colleagues' minds, could be unleashed. Koestler's Law shouts "There is no such thing as an 'uncreative' person, nor is creativity the private reserve of so-called 'creatives.' We can all participate."

But as a statement of a process, Koestler's Law is something of a tease. The examples of music, literature, and life are all very well, but how can we actually apply Koestler's Law in a real business context? In business, where are the patterns? And what are the component parts? Do they exist at all? Where is my "business piano" that I can use to generate as many ideas as I like? Or is Koestler's Law of no practical business value?

As we shall see, Koestler's Law is of enormous practical value, and begins to become so as soon as we realize that, yes, the component parts relevant to business do indeed exist. And their location is . . . *in an existing pattern*! That may sound strange, or even trivial, but a moment's reflection will show that this must be true. If, as we are now agreed, creativity is about finding a new pattern of existing components, then those components must exist now. But where should we look to find them?

The answer to this question emerges as soon as we recognize that, in principle, the individual components from which new patterns can be made can exist in two very different forms: they might exist in a "free," easily accessible, state, like the notes on a piano, or they might exist *bundled together* in an existing pattern, like the notes bundled together in, say, Beethoven's *Fifth Symphony*. In fact, for the components to be readily accessible in a "free" state is rather unusual: far more often, the components are bundled together in existing patterns. And because of the bundling, the individual components themselves are less easily observed, and might at first sight appear to be hidden. The existing patterns, though, are very visible, and the patterns themselves have familiar names: in music, for example, the patterns are called "symphonies," "operas," or "pop songs"; in literature, "novels," "plays," or "poetry"; in chemistry, "molecules"; and in business, "learning," "knowledge," and "experience."

THE NATURE OF LEARNING

We spend our entire life learning, accumulating more knowledge, adding to our experience.

But what is the nature of learning?

Learning enables us to apply an experience of the past into a situation in the future – it builds a "memory" of the future, so whenever we meet a particular set of circumstances, we don't have to work out what to do: we know what to do.

A trivial example of this is getting dressed. This is a process so automatic we no longer even think about it. But imagine what would happen if, each morning, you had to work out how to put on a shirt, how to tie a tie, where to put your shoes. Getting dressed would take literally all day! As indeed it does, as every parent who has ever helped a toddler to do it, knows! But once we've learnt how to do it, we can do it again and again and again, often without conscious thought.

Some learning is about facts – the names of capital cities, chemical formulae, which accounts are usually debits, and which credits. But a lot of learning is about behaviors, about acquiring skills, about solving problems. All learning, however, shares a common characteristic feature: we learn that a particular trigger ("What is the capital of France?," "How do I drive this car?") stimulates a particular response ("Paris," "First I fasten the seat belt, then I check that the gears are in neutral, next I put the key in the ignition. . .").

But how does learning actually work? Here is a model of learning, originally drawn from the work of the Canadian physiologist, Donald Hebb.

Imagine a flat plain; and imagine a raindrop falling on to it. If the landscape is absolutely flat, the raindrop just stays where it lands. But if the landscape is gently undulating, then the raindrop rolls down a slope. This is not a passive process, but an active one – as the raindrop rolls, it carves a very faint depression in the surface, the most rudimentary of valleys. But once this initial depression has been formed, other raindrops falling in the neighborhood are attracted into the valley, and, with each raindrop, the valley becomes more deeply carved, attracting more raindrops, making the valley deeper still . . . until, over long periods of time, the landscape becomes richly carved with a network of mountains, ridges, valleys, and plains, like the Alps, the Rockies, or the Himalayas.

The creation of this landscape is a powerful metaphor for learning. Imagine now a new-born infant. What happens as she experiences the world, and learns how to suck her mother's milk, how to attract attention, how to recognize faces, how to make sounds? If we compare the mind of the new-born infant to a gently undulating plain, then the process of learning is just like the raindrops carving their valleys. And so, over a period of time, as the infant grows into a toddler, a child, a teenager, a young adult, she carves an increasingly rich landscape in her brain, with each "valley" associated with a label such as "sucking Mum's milk," "recognizing Dad's face," "getting dressed," "crossing the road," "playing a particular piece on the piano," "driving an automobile," or whatever.

By the time we become adults, our brains have a uniquely carved, personal landscape – the landscape of our learning, knowledge, and experience.

So, if we want to get dressed in the morning, we zoom down the "getting dressed" valley; if we want to cross the road, we zoom down the "crossing the road" valley; as we drive to work, we are deeply, probably quite unconsciously, in the "driving to work" valley; and as we read our e-mails and prepare for the first meeting of the day, we begin to slide into the "how to manage staff" valley, the "how to negotiate with clients" valley, the "business strategy" valley, or the "why does he always write such stupid e-mails?" valley . . .

This landscape metaphor is real, for recent brain research has established that, during learning, particular brain cells form especially strong connections, enabling these connections to be re-invoked whenever we wish to repeat the learned behavior. Learning is in fact a process of "hard-wiring" our brains!

THE LEARNING TRAP

Learning is immensely valuable, for it means that we don't have to waste time and effort diagnosing a situation and working out what to do whenever the situation might arise. Without having learnt how to cross a road, for example, we'd either stay on the curbstone all day, or be killed by the traffic.

This is fine when we wish to repeat behaviors we have already learnt; but it isn't so fine when we want to do things differently – in particular, when we wish to innovate.

The pull of the valley is very powerful, and we are often sucked into the valley of the familiar, only to become trapped by the known.

If we wish to innovate, we have to find a way to get those raindrops out of the valleys, to unwire those hard-wired brain cells.

> ## WE ARE ALL PRISONERS OF OUR SUCCESS
> The more often you do something – particularly if you are successful at it – the harder it is to find new ways of doing it. We become trapped by familiarity, programmed by habit.
>
> To find new ways of doing things – to innovate – we have to break out of the familiar, we must "unlearn" our habits.
>
> The problem is how.

There is one, and only one, way to escape from the learning trap, to get our raindrops out of our valleys, to unwire our hard-wired brains. And that is to be willing to "unlearn," to be willing to have our learning, knowledge, and experience challenged. That is no easy thing to do, for it is a result of our learning, knowledge, and experience that we have been successful. But there is no escape: if we wish to innovate, we have to unlearn.

Unlearning, however, is very difficult. It's rather like an experienced golfer who decides he wants to improve his swing: his problem is not to learn how to swing properly – it's how to unlearn his current swing.

For before he can learn the correct new action, he has to unlearn, unwind, unravel his old, well-entrenched, bad habits.

But the comparison of the wise manager to the ageing golfer breaks down in one very important respect. The golfer has a problem which he knows he wants to fix. The manager, in contrast, often doesn't have a problem at all – in fact, the manager is usually doing things well and successfully. Which makes doing them innovatively even harder, for to do things innovatively, you must do them differently, which means you must unlearn how you're doing them now. *Even if they're successful.*

It is a fundamental truth that it is extremely rare for innovation in business to take place on genuinely virgin territory, on an open "green-field" site. Rather, innovation almost invariably takes place on very familiar territory indeed – territory we know well, territory on which we have been successful. This familiarity, and the corresponding success, make the process of unlearning especially difficult.

HOW TO UNLEARN

We can now see that creativity in business requires two distinct, and separate, activities: one is to discover something new, and most people find that exhilarating; the other is to unlearn the old, and most people find that very difficult. This, of course, is the reason why younger people (and indeed children) are often regarded as more creative and innovative than older folk: younger people have had less opportunity to learn, to gain experience, to hard-wire their brains. As a consequence, they have less unlearning to do, and so they find it easier. Older people, who have more experience and learning, just have that much more to unlearn, and have to deal with the emotional anguish of letting go of the past – but once they can come to terms with that, then discovering the new is no problem at all.

Accordingly, the tools and techniques for creativity – including all of the 250 techniques identified by Arthur VanGundy in his book *Techniques of Structured Problem Solving* (see page 23) – are mechanisms to help you unlearn.

Springboards and retro-fits

In my view, the great variety of tools and techniques for creativity fall into two main categories, which I call ***springboards*** and ***retro-fits***. Let me explain these in terms of the landscape metaphor.

Suppose we are in the leisure industry, and we wish to generate some new ideas for, say, a new restaurant concept. There we are, stuck in our "valley" representing the-way-we-run-restaurants-now, desperately trying to escape into another valley, the rich new valley of a brand new concept for a restaurant chain. The *springboard* techniques take, as their starting point, *knowledge of what you do now*, and use this knowledge as a "springboard" to new ideas, thus navigating you out of an existing "valley" into a new one. In contrast, the *retro-fit* techniques *project your mind to a distant "valley,"* and offer the opportunity of discovering a path back from that distant valley to where you are now.

This probably sounds rather obscure, so let me make things real by providing two examples: my own process, ***InnovAction!***, as a springboard, and the *random word* process as a retro-fit.

InnovAction!

InnovAction! is my own process, which can help you unlearn, and, as a consequence, help you discover a myriad of new ideas. Somewhat surprisingly, the basis of ***InnovAction!***, the key to unlearning, is to rejoice in what you already know!

INNOVACTION!

InnovAction! is a six-step process to make idea generation deliberate and systematic.

Step 1 – Define the focus of attention. The first step is to define the area in which you wish to innovate – the focus of attention. In general, a narrower focus ("Let's invent some new restaurant formats") is preferable to a wider one ("Let's invent a new leisure concept").

Step 2 – Define what you know. Having defined the focus of attention, document, as a series of bullet points, what you know about the topic, its characteristics and features, all the assumptions you make about it ("Restaurants have a chef ..."). You can do this alone, but if you are doing this as part of a group, do this step by yourself, in silence, without consulting colleagues.

Step 3 – Share. Now share your list with your colleagues, and compile an aggregate list of characteristics, features, and assumptions.

Step 4 – Ask "How might this be different?" Choose one of the features from the list, and ask "How might this be different?"

Step 5 – Let it be. Then let the conversation go ... you will be amazed by what happens.

Step 6 – Then choose another feature. When the discussion on the first feature starts to lose energy, go back to the list of features compiled in Step 3, choose another, and proceed with Steps 4 and 5. Cycle around Steps 4 and 5 for no more than three hours.

So, let's suppose that our "focus of attention" is to invent some new formats for a restaurant – that's Step 1. Step 2 is define everything we know about restaurants as a series of bullet points, and share our lists with those of our colleagues (Step 3), as shown in Table 6.1.

Table 6.1 Everything we know about restaurants.

» It's a place where you enjoy food ...
» ... and drink (alcoholic or not)
» You can book a table in advance
» Usually, diners take their cars
» It's convivial
» There is attractive décor, furnishings and furniture
» There is a pleasant environment for socializing
» Staff are friendly
» Service is efficient
» You can buy drinks as well as food
» Children can be welcome or unwelcome
» You choose your food from a menu
» There is a wine list
» There are tables and chairs and a seating arrangement
» You are served by a waiter or a waitress
» The food is served on crockery
» There is a chef
» Sometimes you wait in a waiting area
» Starters are before the main course, then you have the dessert
» There are many different types: themed by nationality or type of cuisine ...
» ... or by its décor or style ...
» ... sit-down or take-away ...
» ... elegant or fast-food ...

Table 6.1 (*Continued*).

» ... with a choice of food or a fixed menu
» The restaurant provide plates and glasses ...
» ... and cutlery, all laid out as a place setting
» There is a menu
» You choose the food you want
» Some restaurants are good value for money ...
» ... others are expensive, and you go there for status or to be seen
» The hours of opening usually correspond to meals
» Sometimes you book ... sometimes not
» A waiter or waitress usually serves you ...
» ... but some restaurants are self-service
» The chef cooks for you
» The chef is in a kitchen
» The chef is not usually seen, but you may know who the chef is
» Sometimes you bring your own wine
» Restaurants employ staff
» You pay for your meal – with cash, checks, credit cards
» You go there when you are hungry

» You go there to entertain business associates
» You go there to celebrate
» The restaurant might have entertainment
» The ambience, music, lighting is often a feature ...
» ... as is the location
» The restaurant might be indoors ... or out
» It may be stand-alone ... or part of a chain ... or a franchise
» The restaurant should be easy to get to
» It may also have accommodation
» When you sit down at the table, you stay seated
» You sit with the people you go with
» Restaurants often advertise
» You go there for special occasions
» The restaurant is comfortable
» There are smoking and non-smoking areas
» There are restrooms
» There is a parking lot
» You travel there
» Staff canteens are restaurants too
» Restaurants are clean and hygienic
» Restaurants build a reputation
» You pay for the food and drink

This list is drawn from the workshops I run with clients, and is a typical example: the items are in no particular order, and they range over all aspects of a restaurant's function and operation. The list is not, in any sense, complete, for I am sure that you can think of many features of a restaurant not mentioned here; you may even disagree with some of those in the list. No matter: these features represent the features that many people perceive – and, importantly, they represent the ''view'' that these people have had when they ''stand in their valleys, labeled restaurants,'' and look around.

Step 4 is the key step. We take any of the bullet points, and ask ''How might this be different?''

So, for example, take the point ''There is a chef.'' How might this be different? Hey – that's really silly! Of course there's a chef! It can't be different!! Well, pause a while. For sure restaurants usually have chefs, and this is the familiar ''valley'' of our experience. If we want to generate new ideas, we must escape from our familiar valleys; we have to ''drag the raindrop'' from the valley floor on to a neighboring ridge; we have to unwire our hard-wired brains. So the jolt we all experience when we are faced with when asking the question ''How might this be different?'' is perfectly natural – it is the act of getting the raindrop out of that valley, the act of unwiring our brains.

Well, one way of ''There is a chef'' being different is if there were no chef at all. And if there were no chef at all, how could this restaurant operate? Perhaps *we* are the chef: so it might be a restaurant that was themed around barbecues, so everyone brings their own food, and cooks it on grills provided around picnic tables; alternatively, the restaurant might provide the food too, so people can choose what they prefer to eat.

Wait a moment. The concept of people cooking their own food stimulates another idea. Suppose that people cook their own food, but under the supervision of a master chef – this restaurant could be a place where people can get expert coaching. In this case, the restaurant still has a chef – but the chef is playing a different role: rather than being the person who cooks the food, this chef is acting as a teacher. Maybe there is a restaurant themed around getting expert tuition. . .

This is in fact a demonstration of Step 5–Let it be, for as we explore the consequences of asking ''How might this be different?'' of the feature ''There is a chef,'' we soon discover all sorts of very plausible ideas – the barbecue restaurant, the restaurant as cookery school ... And remember, that at this stage, we are in the innermost zone of the Innovation Target, that of idea generation. We are avoiding the quick rush to judgment of premature evaluation, and we are making no statements as to whether or not the barbecue theme, the cookery school theme, or any other theme is a "good" or "bad" idea. At this stage, they are just ideas, and the more ideas we have, the better. Later, we can move into the zone of evaluation, and assess the ideas for their business merit. But at the moment, we are letting it be. . .

"There is a chef." How might that be different? Perhaps there is not *a* chef, but lots of them. That seems to imply a very big restaurant, for if we were to employ lots of chefs, we would need to have lots of customers. Would we? There are (at least) two different ways of employing lots of chefs: one is to have lots of chefs cooking at the same time, for lots of customers; but another is to have lots of chefs, one at a time. One at a time? How would that work? Mmm. The chefs might be on duty for, say, a week at a time. How could we organize that? And why would they do that? What other people behave in this way, working for a week at a time?

Pop stars. Conductors. Opera singers. They work for a week (or even a day) at a time in *any one location*. So, what about a restaurant featuring "the celebrity chef of the month?" This restaurant could have many chefs, but each is present only for a limited amount of time. And if many of them are celebrity chefs, then the restaurant could bring the greatest food in the world to its locality by bringing the celebrity chefs "on tour." Yes, it probably is true that, at the moment, chefs don't behave like that, even the famous ones. Why not? Maybe because they've never had the incentive, maybe because they've never been approached to do so. Maybe there is an opportunity for someone to start a business as an "impresario of chefs," co-ordinating world tours of celebrity chefs, just as theatrical impresarios organize tours of pop stars and opera singers?

I think I'm running out of steam a bit now. Let's invoke Step 6–Then choose another feature. Let's take "There is a menu." How might this be different? What if there were no menu?

Now that, surely, must be crazy. Of course there must be a menu! How else would a customer know what was on offer, and know what to choose?

Well, maybe the restaurant doesn't offer any choice, so everybody gets whatever the chef is making. But maybe the restaurant does know what you want. Eh? How would the restaurant know what you wanted before you go there? Easy – because you've been there before, maybe many times. Indeed, every time you've been there, the restaurant has produced an itemized bill, specifying exactly what you ate. But what does the restaurant do with that information? Probably the same as you do with the bill – throw it away (assuming you're not keeping it to claim against tax, that is!). Yes, the restaurant will keep a record of the sales value (for their accounting), but they probably throw away the detail. Oh dear. What a waste. My local Italian restaurant really should know that I just love fresh asparagus. And if they were to phone me early in the week and say, "Hey, Mr Sherwood, we have a great order of the most fantastic asparagus coming in next Saturday morning. Can we book a table for you and your wife for 8.30 that evening?," there's quite a chance that I'd say "Yes, what a great idea!" So my wife and I have a nice meal, and the restaurant pre-books my table and takes control of the booking process – rather than waiting for me to call them, they call me ... Now that idea is not, repeat not, crazy. That's what customer relationship management means for a restaurant. And they have all the information they need – they've been collecting it for years. Or have they? Once again, it's all about new patterns of existing component parts ...

HOW – AND WHY – INNOVACTION! WORKS

Take a moment to read the last few pages again, and look at the ideas we discovered. Barbecue restaurants. Restaurants for teaching or coaching. Celebrity chef restaurants. Restaurants that already know what I like. Restaurants that take control of the booking process. That's five quite different ideas in a matter of minutes. And we've only just started, for we took only two features of the list on page 50 – "There is a chef" and "There is a menu." Imagine how many additional ideas we could generate if we went down the list, item by item, systematically asking "How might this be different?"

So let's see how, and why, that happened.

Our focus of attention is to discover new formats for a restaurant (Step 1), and our starting point was to list the features, as a series of bullet points, of restaurants-as-we-know-them-today. That was Step 2, and a representative list of features is shown in Table 6.1 on pages 50–1, as represented symbolically in the left-hand column of Table 6.2.

Table 6.2   Features of existing and future restaurants.

Features of restaurants-as-we-know-them-today	Features of the-restaurant-of-tomorrow
» xxxxxxxxxxxxxxxxxxxxxx	» xxxxxxxxxxxxxxxxxxxxxx
» xxxxxxxxxxxxxxxxxxxxxx	» xxxxxxxxxxxxxxxxxxxxxx
» xxxxxxxxxxxxxxxxxxxxxx	» qqqqqqqqqqqqqqqqqqqqqq
» xxxxxxxxxxxxxxxxxxxxxx	» xxxxxxxxxxxxxxxxxxxxxx
» xxxxxxxxxxxxxxxxxxxxxx	» xxxxxxxxxxxxxxxxxxxxxx
» xxxxxxxxxxxxxxxxxxxxxx	» xxxxxxxxxxxxxxxxxxxxxx
» xxxxxxxxxxxxxxxxxxxxxx	» xxxxxxxxxxxxxxxxxxxxxx

Imagine, for a moment, that you were describing the features of a new form of restaurant, as indicated in the right-hand column of Table 6.2. What would that list look like? And how would you distinguish it from the list describing restaurants-as-we-know-them-today?

If you compare these two lists, you notice something very important: the two lists are *different* as regards at least one feature – in this instance, the feature now indicated as qqqqq. This, of course, is quite obvious: if the two lists were identical, the two forms of restaurant being described would also be identical and indistinguishable. But since the second list describes something new, this list must, at least in part, be different from the first list.

That which is new must, necessarily, be different from what exists now.

This self-evident truth is the essence of the *InnovAction!* process. In *InnovAction!*, for any given focus of attention, we start with the list of features of the world-as-it-is-now, as shown in the left-hand column of the table, and the right-hand side is of course blank. We then select one of the features from the left-hand column, and deliberately ask the question "How might this be different?", in that way forcing us to discover some different feature, forcing us into the right-hand column. And you saw what happened – ideas tumble along, one after the other.

At this point, it is important to recognize that although the statement "that which is new must, necessarily, be different from what exists now" is fundamentally true, it doesn't necessarily work the other way around. "That which is different must be new" is a false statement, not a true one, and it might be thought that searching for differences from the *status quo* is a waste of time. Well, that's a good and valid point. But, in practice, my experience is that it just doesn't work that way at all. Asking "How might this be different?" can certainly take you into old or familiar territory, but it also takes you exactly where you want to go - into new territory where neither you nor perhaps anyone else has been before. Perhaps someone else has already invented a barbecue restaurant. Or maybe someone else is already a "chef impresario." That needn't necessarily stop you from creating an even better barbecue restaurant, or being a more successful chef impresario; either way, these are issues of evaluation, not idea generation. At this stage, all ideas are valuable. And by asking "How might this be different?," and letting it be, you never know what you might discover. . .

In terms of the landscape metaphor, the focus of attention (Step 1), in this case restaurants, sends our minds down a particular valley, the valley labeled "restaurants." Then, the process of defining what we know about restaurants in terms of a list of bullet points (Step 2) encourages us "to stand at the bottom of the valley, and describe in detail what we see." Since different people often have different perceptions of the same subject, Step 3–Share, enables the features of "your" valley to be combined with the features of other people's valleys, thus enabling you to compile an aggregate list of features of the combined valleys.

The purpose of the next step, "How might this be different?," is then to get the "raindrop out of the valley," forcing your thinking out of the learning trap, pushing the "raindrop" up the slope to a neighboring "ridge." This often feels strange and uncomfortable, and, just as gravity is always trying to pull the raindrop back into the valley, our "common sense" is always telling us "Of course, restaurants always have a chef," or "Don't be crazy! A restaurant must have a menu!" But, with a little practice and the building of some confidence, you soon get used to living in the world of restaurants without chefs, as that raindrop totters precariously on that ridge. That's Step 5–Let it be. And then, all of a sudden, the raindrop falls into a new valley. The valley of the barbecue restaurant. The valley of the celebrity guest chef. The valley of the restaurant that takes control of the booking process. And we've discovered a host of new ideas.

And then, when we have run out of steam, we can ask "How might this be different?" of another feature, and drag another raindrop out of the valley. And we can do this again and again and again, for, with a large list of bullet points in the description of the world-as-it-is-today, we have a wealth of features to use as raw material.

InnovAction! also makes sense in terms of Koestler's Law. We start off with an existing pattern – "restaurants-as-we-know-them-today." We then disaggregate this pattern to reveal its components (Step 2), and combine our descriptions with the descriptions of our colleagues. Then "How might this be different?" triggers a process of searching for new patterns, drawing in components from the outside as well as from the focus of attention – the fact that pop stars and opera singers go on tour was a "component" from outside the restaurant business that can be combined with existing aspects of a restaurant to form a new pattern.

As Koestler's Law states, it's all about finding new patterns of existing components, and the more familiar the parts, the more striking the new whole.

When you use *InnovAction!*, your starting point is very firmly what you know – as expressed in the series of bullet points describing the focus of attention. By asking "How might this be different?" of any given feature, you are using this feature as a springboard to leap from the known to the new. The only requirement for using *InnovAction!* is some knowledge – you have to have the springboard to start with. But once you have that, the magic question "How might this be different?" can springboard you to places you never dreamed of. And if you do this with a small group, you springboard off one another's ideas too – brain bank connectivity (see page 35) for real!

This is very different from conventional brainstorming, which typically starts with a blank sheet of paper. My experience of brainstorming is that it can very quickly run dry. There is of course a reason for this – there are no triggers. But with *InnovAction!*, you are not starting with a blank sheet of paper: on the contrary, you are starting with a very full sheet of paper indeed – a sheet of paper which reflects your own, and your colleagues', collective knowledge, learning and experience. So rejoice in that, and use it as a springboard to discover all sorts of wonderful new ideas.

You'll find a lot more about ***InnovAction!*** in my book *Smart Things to Know About Innovation and Creativity* – but let's now move on to the other major category of idea generation processes, the retro-fits.

Retro-fits

An example of a retro-fit method for idea generation is the "random word" process, which works like this:

» Choose a focus of attention.
» Choose a genuinely random word, perhaps by opening a dictionary, perhaps by looking in a newspaper.
» Compile a list of words generated by word association from the trigger word.
» Then see if any of the words on the list suggest a new idea related to the focus of attention.

Let's keep our focus of attention as the creation of some new restaurant formats, and we'll choose "mirror" as the random word.

Table 6.3 shows my list starting from "mirror":

When you do this, you don't have to link all your words back the original trigger – in fact, the list may be a whole sequence of random words which have nothing to do with each other at all. Most people, however, use one word as a bridge to another in all sorts of ways – mirrors are for looking into, so that suggests "look," "reflect," "see"; "see" sounds like "sea," so that can lead to "ship," "boat," float"; this might trigger a rhyme with "goat" leading to names of animals... The list can evolve in a myriad of ways, especially if done in a small group.

You can see how my mind is working (any psychiatrists reading this, please don't despair!): the flow through animals led to big things; a short while ago, I had a conversation about Roald Dahl's book *The Big Friendly Giant*; wasn't there a Hitchcock film called *Notorious* which starred Ingrid Bergman?; *Z Cars* was a long-running police series on BBC television in the 1960s; and somewhere in my mind is the name – a

Table 6.3 My results of the random word process, starting from "mirror".

» look	» famous	» clean
» reflect	» infamous	» wash
» see	» criminal	» washing powder
» sea	» notorious	» supermarket
» ship	» Ingrid	» shopping trolley
» boat	Bergman	» bus
» float	» Casablanca	» train
» goat	» Africa	» teach
» elephant	» Zulu	» educate
» big	» *Z Cars*	» student
» huge	» television	» school-boy
» giant	» movie	» short trousers
» friendly	» theater	» short skirts
» happy	» theatricality	» knees
» celebration	» showmanship	» legs
» celebrity	» soap opera	» diamonds
	» soap	

prohibition era gangster, I think – "Legs" Diamond. Also, the process isn't linear – when I put down "soap opera," my mind had drifted back to "television."

So, does this list trigger any thoughts about – ah, yes, that was it – restaurants?

Well, let's take "Legs" Diamond. He was (I think) a gangster. So what about a chain of pizza restaurants, themed on Chicago in the 1920s? The waiters could be dressed up as hoods, and the waitresses as speak-easy girls; the pizzas could have names like "Al Capone Special," "Nitty Gritty" and "Elliot Ness Monster"; there could be screens (see the trigger "television?") around the restaurant showing clips of gangster movies like *White Heat*, *The Roaring Twenties*, *Some Like it Hot*, *The Sting*... For a touch of theater (another word on the list), you could even imagine a fake police raid (that's there too, implicit in *Z Cars*) from time to time to liven things up! And what about *Pizza Nostra* as the name of the chain?

There's another theme running through the list, as a sort of undercurrent, of celebrity and show. What about a restaurant which does not have small tables for couples and foursomes, but has big, round tables, seating about twelve? You wouldn't go to a restaurant like that to have an intimate conversation with a loved one – you'd be seated with strangers. But what if those strangers were people you actually wanted to meet – celebrities? Can you imagine a restaurant which advertised "Book now to meet next month's celebrity guests" – maybe there would be four or five tables, each with a celebrity from entertainment, maybe a sports star, a journalist, a novelist, whatever? Every month, the restaurant could line up a different list of celebrities, and – provided the celebrities didn't object to being "on show" for the evening in this kind of context (some celebrities would love it), that would draw the crowds.

Speaking of celebrities, there is one celebrity in a restaurant who is often overlooked – the chef. What about a restaurant that advertises "Celebrity chef of the month?" What I have in mind here is a bit like pop stars and opera singers who go on tour. One of the benefits of this is that a much wider population sees the star live, and the star earns quite a tidy sum too. What about someone acting as an impresario, orchestrating tours of the leading chefs, so that diners in New York, London, Paris, and Copenhagen can enjoy the food of the world's master chefs in their own city?

Now the concept of people travelling (the chefs to the restaurants around the world, in that case), combined with the word, television, triggers another thought. Let's wrap that together with "celebration" and "happy." It so happens I'm writing this a couple of days before my younger son's eleventh birthday, and one of the treats he really enjoys is a celebratory birthday meal at a restaurant. For occasions like birthdays and anniversaries, you don't want a table just for two, because it's really nice to have family and friends together. But one reason they often can't be together is because they live a long way away – overseas, perhaps.

So what about a network of restaurants, around the world, with Web-cameras and TV screens, linked by the Internet – a sort of social video conferencing? That way I could celebrate with family and friends in all sorts of locations at the same time. It's not quite as good as all being together in the same place, but it's a lot better than not being together at all. Who will be the first to open a chain of e-restaurants?

Going back to the list, let me pick up "supermarket" and "shopping trolley." Sometimes I find shopping fun, sometimes it's a chore. Many supermarkets have a coffee shop where you can take a break, and rest those tired feet. But I haven't ever experienced a coffee shop where I can sit down, and then someone says to me "Welcome to our supermarket. Please enjoy our complimentary cappuccino and croissant/tea and muffin/whatever. My name is Amanda, and I am your personal shopper. Please give me your shopping list, and I will wheel the trolley around and collect everything you need. I'll be back in about twenty minutes so you can check everything is OK, and our electronic trolley will automatically total everything up. When you're happy, you can pay me, here at your table, by credit card/loyalty card/cash/check/whatever, and then I'll wheel the trolley to your car." That's a different sort of restaurant too.

You get the idea: the list of words produced from the original random trigger acts as a seed for new ideas.

How does this work? Well, if we go back to our landscape, raindrop-in-the-valley metaphor, our focus of attention (restaurants, in the case) takes us down our mental valley labeled "restaurants." The random word – and it really doesn't matter what it is (if you remember, I chose "mirror" – in fact because I happened to be looking into one whilst I was thinking about this) – pitches your mind into a totally different place, which has nothing whatsoever to do with the focus of attention. It's as if you threw a ball as far as possible in your mental landscape, and it happens to roll into a distant, unrelated valley, such as "mirror."

Then, as you stand in the distant valley ("mirror"), the word association process invites you to look around and see what other "valleys" you can identify, in whatever direction you happen to scan. And, very quickly, your mind goes from valley to valley, skirting ridges, noticing peaks, helter-skelter through your mental landscape. And if you do this in a small group, everyone is going in different directions, and it becomes quite impossible for a facilitator to write it all down!

After a few minutes of this, and a list of, say, 30–50 words, you will find that you have scanned a huge amount of your mental landscape, totally freely, to the extent that you can often forget what the original focus of attention was!

The next stage is to "stand" in these distant valleys, and "look back" towards the focus of attention, and see if anything pops into your mind. In this way, the random word process is "retro-fitting" possible trial solutions (solutions associated with concepts such as supermarkets or celebrities) to the original question "What themes can I generate for a new restaurant format?" This is in contrast to the *InnovAction!* process, in which you start from everything you know about restaurants, and use this as a springboard to new ideas.

A very important point is that springboards and retro-fits are not mutually exclusive – the same ideas are potentially accessible from both starting points, and can be discovered working either "forwards" or "backwards." You will have noticed, for example, that the "celebrity chef" idea emerged from the *InnovAction!* process by asking "How might this be different?" of the feature "There is a chef"; the same idea was generated through the random word process as triggered by "celebrity."

InnovAction!, which springboards from what you know to what you might know, can therefore result in ideas which are very similar, or identical, to those generated by a process such as random words, which encourages you to retro-fit from a series of possible trial solutions back to the original focus of attention. Although the results can be the same, the processes are very different: *InnovAction!* starts on the very solid ground of the known, and moves you to the unknown; the use of random words pitches you directly into the unknown, and then encourages you to work backwards from a variety of different potential possibilities.

In my experience, some people just love the "retro-fit" techniques, and are amazingly good at using them. I don't have the data to prove it, but I suspect that these are the people who perceive themselves to be "creative", and who are regarded by their colleagues as such. It's no accident that the random word technique is beloved by advertising agencies – it is a very powerful method for creating metaphors, and much advertising is based on explicit or implicit metaphor. It is also the stock-in-trade of comedians, and we all marvel at those who can make great jokes by bringing together seemingly distant concepts.

LATERAL THINKING

Everyone has heard of lateral thinking, and, as its originator, Edward de Bono, not infrequently points out, the phrase is now to be found in the Oxford English Dictionary, and so is officially part of the English language.

De Bono coined the term in his book *Lateral Thinking for Management*, first published in 1967; as with all innovations, lateral thinking is itself a new pattern formed from existing parts, not least of which is the name – in *The Act of Creation*, published in 1964, Arthur Koestler refers to a process which he calls "thinking aside".

Lateral thinking, thinking aside, ***InnovAction!***: all are names for particular processes which share a common objective – to provide a mechanism to aid the process of unlearning, and for the discovery of new patterns; all have their own distinctive methods.

Central to lateral thinking is a new word, "po," invented by de Bono and standing for "provocative operation". To see how this is used, let's take one of de Bono's own examples, which he expresses as "Po: planes land upside down."

In everyday language, this means "As a way of provoking new thoughts, let's consider what happens if planes land upside down." If this were to happen, as well as having all the drinks spill, and the passengers feeling odd, the pilot, though ostensibly upside down, would have a good view of the ground when the plane is landing, and also when taking off. This makes a lot of sense, and I'm sure we'd all agree that it is a "good thing" for aircraft pilots to have as good a view of the ground as possible when landing and taking off. And, come to think of it, the pilot of a plane the size of a jumbo jet couldn't be sitting in a more unhelpful place, perched on top of a hugely bulbous nose-cone, with a perfect view of the sky above, but a 100% obscured view of the ground below. Aha – what a great idea! Have pilots sitting, the right way up of course, in a capsule underneath the plane, so that the plane still flies the right way up, but the pilot can now see what is going on as the plane lands or takes off. Alternatively, have two positions for the pilot, one on top for general flying, the other underneath for take-offs and landings; or, at the very least, have a video camera which projects an image of the ground into the cockpit. Any of these ideas has got to make more sense, be cheaper, and be easier to engineer, than the solution developed by the designers of Concorde. Their way of making sure that the pilot can see the ground on landing is to have the entire nose assembly of the aircraft dip down. A video camera has to be cheaper.

Po, the provocative operation, provokes and shocks our thinking to consider the unthinkable – what happens if planes land upside down? And if we reflect on this, and – my language this time – let it be, then our raindrops, wrenched out of their valley by being po'd, discover the bright new valley of innovation.

Many of the examples cited in de Bono's various books are dramatic and startling. One notable one is "Po: a factory is downstream of itself." This translates to "As a way of stimulating your thinking, consider what might happen if a factory, which is situated by a river and uses the river water for its manufacturing process, is sited downstream of itself." When I first read this one, it made my brain hurt, but once I got my mind around it, I was able to follow de Bono's explanation that one consequence of this would be that the factory is obliged to take its own effluent into its intake pipes. At first sight, this is not a good thing, for the "downstream" factory is being polluted by its "upstream" ghost. It can become a good thing, however, if the "upstream" ghost cleans its own effluent before discharging it into the river.

This suggests that a regulator, or government agency concerned about the environment, could take the very simple measure of introducing a law to force all river-sited factories to discharge their effluent upstream of their intake pipes. The factory as a whole is sited in a perfectly normal way, and all that is different is the relative siting of the intake (downstream) and effluent (upstream) pipes. Once again, a somewhat bizarre "po" has forced the raindrops out of the valley (almost literally in this case), and some exploratory thought has discovered a valid and practical new idea.

There is no doubt that de Bono has written a lot of very good stuff, and he has been an enormously successful evangelist. But the difficulty I had when reading many of his books was the question "Where does 'po' come from?" – de Bono seemed to me to be producing the various "po's" like rabbits from a hat. Each of them had a wonderful story, but I was left with thinking that it probably was as hard to discover the right "po" as it was to have a good new idea in the first place. Maybe

I didn't read de Bono's books carefully enough, but it seemed to me that rather than solving the problem of how to generate new ideas systematically and safely, "po" just pushed the problem back one stage from discovering a new idea to discovering the right "po."

And that's the key difference, I believe, between *InnovAction!* and lateral thinking. *InnovAction!* has a very specific and well-defined starting point – what you know, as expressed in that now-familiar list of bullet points (Table 6.2). It isn't a blank sheet of paper, and it isn't arbitrary. It isn't magic, and it isn't luck. It's what you know. Once you've got that list of bullet points, you can then ask "How might this be different?," and springboard from there, as we have now seen with the many examples in this chapter.

InnovAction!'s "How might this be different?" is, in fact, doing much the same job as de Bono's "po," for the exploration process from there is very similar. But whereas de Bono is not – to my mind anyway – very clear on where the "po's" come from, I am crystal clear on where the "How might this be different?"'s come from – they come from your learning.

Indeed, if we go back to the two de Bono examples, we can see how the two processes converge. De Bono's "Po: planes land upside down" would map on to Table 6.2's list of bullet points describing planes-as-they-are-today as the feature "planes land the right way up" – one of those obvious-but-true descriptions of the way-things-are-today that are so hard to notice. How might this be different? Well, they might land upside down, and we go from there. A bit further down (or, more likely up) the list of bullet points in *InnovAction!*, though, you are quite likely to find "the pilot sits in a cockpit above the nose-cone." How might this be different? Well ... he might sit somewhere else ... actually in the nose-cone, or right at the front, or underneath perhaps. And maybe the "good idea" is discovered rather more directly.

Likewise, if we take "Po: a factory is downstream of itself," then the list of bullet points of riverside-factories-as-we-know-them-today might include (if we had been thorough enough) "effluent is usually discharged downstream." How might this be different? What if the effluent were discharged upstream? Aha. This example makes an important point. It could be that we never noticed the feature "effluent is usually discharged downstream" – it is both self-evident, and in many ways not something we would readily spot. But as soon as we do notice it, and ask "How might this be different?," we discover a new and important idea. The moral here is: the richer and more perceptive the list of features of the world-as-it-is-today, the more likely you are to find that special differentiating feature.

So, you should definitely read de Bono, especially *Lateral Thinking for Managers*, and *Serious Creativity*: then take a view as to which process you prefer, or indeed, mix and match the pieces as you like. As Koestler said (again!), it's all about new patterns of existing components.

TIME TO REFLECT

Well, this has been a long chapter, but I trust an invigorating one. Although, as we saw in our discussion of the Innovation Target, innovation comprises the four stages of idea generation, evaluation, development, and implementation, the heart of the process is idea generation. If you are not creative, if you have no new ideas, then the rest is sunk.

Creativity and idea generation are often also mystical, mythical, and misunderstood. But I trust that now the mystery is explained, the myths are debunked, and you really understand.

IDEA GENERATION – THE KEY PRINCIPLES

» Koestler's Law states that creativity – the generation of new ideas – is not a matter of luck or genius. Rather, it can be made to happen by a deliberate process of searching for new patterns of existing components.

» For innovation in business, the components that need to be recombined to form the new patterns are not laid bare, like the notes on a piano. Rather, they exist bundled together in existing patterns – the patterns of our knowledge, learning, and experience.

» As a consequence, before a new pattern can be formed, the old patterns need to be broken apart – only then can the component parts be uncovered and made available for new pattern formation.

» This process of breaking apart our knowledge, learning, and experience is one of *unlearning*. Most people find unlearning very difficult to do, especially when we have been successful in working the "old way".

» All the tools and techniques of creativity are mechanisms to help you unlearn. In general, these tools fall into two categories – *springboards* and *retro-fits*.

» Springboards are processes which take as the starting point your existing knowledge, learning and experience. The ***InnovAction!*** process, for example, takes this, identifies the underlying elements, and uses the question "How might this be different?" to discover new ideas.

» Retro-fits, such as the random word technique, project your imagination into a different domain, and encourage you to discover new ideas by retro-fitting from the different domain back to the focus of attention.

Innovation in Practice

This chapter presents four case studies of the *InnovAction!* process in action at: the utility, Yorkshire Electricity; the educational establishment, Oakham School; the foods giant, Nestlé; and the media company, Pearson Television.

Does systematic idea generation actually work in practice?

Yes. It does. So, in addition to the many examples of the last chapter, here are four case studies based on my client experience. I would like to take this opportunity to thank Yorkshire Electricity, Oakham School, Nestlé and Pearson Television for their permission to publish these cases.

YORKSHIRE ELECTRICITY – COST-EFFECTIVE IT

An issue faced by many companies is to ensure the cost-effectiveness of its information technology (IT) function. This was the theme of a very productive workshop run with Yorkshire Electricity, one of the UK's privatized utilities. Amongst the (very long) list of bullet points describing the world-as-it-is-now were these two:

» We develop new computer applications for the business, and we also support the applications after they are implemented.
» We are a cost center within the business.

"How can we be more cost-effective in providing support to live applications?" was selected as a "focus of attention" for the *Innov-Action!* process, and this was combined with asking "How might this be different?" of the point "We are a cost center within the business."

If we aren't a cost center within the business, what else might we be? Well, we might be a profit center (this led to a number of ideas about how the IT department might generate revenue); or we might be a separate business altogether, with the utility business as a client (leading to ideas about a buy-out); alternatively, we might be owned by someone else. Who might that be? Perhaps it might be another organization that specializes in service, such as a company that helps motorists who have broken down at the roadside, such as the UK organizations the AA or the RAC.

This led the group to compile a list of bullet points about how the AA and the RAC provide their service, including:

» There is a one-off annual fee.
» There is a price list, offering different levels of service for different levels of fee.
» Service levels are published.
» Failed service levels attract penalties.

» The service provider sometimes sub-contracts work to local garages.
» Membership is held on a database.
» The person is covered, not the car.

This comparison triggered a number of ideas:

» *Pricing*: there were a number of ideas about changing the internal transfer pricing structure so that different prices correspond to different levels of service, thus providing users with a good understanding of the true costs of different types of IT support, but without becoming bureaucratic.

» *Service levels*: there are already a series of service level agreements, but these were formulated some time ago. In the spirit of "constructive restlessness," the group agreed it would be very helpful to look through these to ensure that they are fully fit-for-purpose, including the possibility of penalties.

» *Sub-contracting*: could we use local sub-contactors, especially to support locations distant from the call center?

» *Customer databases*: amongst their large user community, there is a wide diversity in IT skills, and some users require much more support than others. Perhaps those who use the support service much more often should be charged more; or perhaps they should be invited to tailored training programs, so they can be more confident in their use of IT systems.

» *The person not the car*: this led to a discussion about how the support service could be tailored much more personally to each user, and then one person in the group proposed the raindrop-shaker "What if each user had their own personal support consultant?" One way of doing this might be to recruit a lot more people, so that each consultant would sit alongside each user, but you don't have to do it that way. What about a "virtual" consultant, providing the "help" service on-screen – just like a tailored version of the on-screen helpers provided with Microsoft, but fully knowledgeable about the business's applications, and even the user herself?

Key learning

The issue being tackled by Yorkshire Electricity – the cost-effectiveness of IT – is very familiar. Every organization faces this issue, and every organization faces this issue in every aspect of its business. This is therefore a powerful example of the fact that innovation in business never takes place on a green-field site.

Despite the familiarity of the focus of attention, the process of unlearning, and using ***InnovAction!*** as a springboard to discover new ideas, was immensely successful.

OAKHAM SCHOOL – AN INNOVATIVE TEACHING AND LEARNING ENVIRONMENT

"Chaos!"

"A riot!"

"It'll be like Lord of the Flies!"

"Mayhem!"

I'd seen these words on a flip-chart from across the room, so I wandered over to eavesdrop on the conversation. I was in a conference center with a group of teachers and trustees from Oakham School, in Rutland, England's smallest county. The school teaches about 1000 children – 500 boys, 500 girls; 500 boarders, 500 day pupils – aged between 11 and 18, and has a reputation as one of the most forward-thinking schools in the UK. For some months, the school had been in discussions with a charity concerning the possibility of funding for a new building, and this had given the headmaster, Tony Little, the idea that it might become a center for innovative learning and teaching. Oakham School was founded in 1584, and a moment's thought will convince you that, fundamentally, teaching has changed little since those days in which the pupils sat at a master's feet – possibly at that time a monk – and sought to remember his words of wisdom. Yes, the technology has evolved somewhat – the increasing use of print has saved a lot of manual labor, and whiteboards and overhead projectors have replaced blackboards and chalk. But the process is probably sufficiently similar that a pupil time-traveler, teleported from Oakham in 1584 to Oakham in 2000, would probably recognize where he had landed.

At the top of the list of the bullet points describing "the classroom experience," the selected focus of attention was "there is a teacher." How might this be different? Well, suppose there is no teacher . . . and you arrive at the words I quoted at the start of this section.

Let me pick up the discussion from John Fern, a historian:

"Wait a moment, folks. Our kids really aren't that irresponsible. They often carry out lots of tasks without minute-to-minute supervision."

"Yes, they do a lot of project work, which they really enjoy. Let's make this a bit more concrete. Suppose we take something we do already – like preparing a debate. And let's suppose further that we were to give the kids a whole day to use the new building to do just that. But with no teachers inside the building at the same time. How would we organize that?"

"There would have to be some really good preparation, so the kids had a series of well-defined and appropriate tasks."

"And were organized in teams to do them. . ."

". . .maybe with some people directly working on the specific task of preparing the debate, but maybe others doing research, or preparing materials, or even making a record of the process itself. . ."

"And if anyone did need some help, maybe there could be a Web-camera or something, so that we could be contacted. That way, we're not actually in the building, but the kids aren't cut off if they really do need help."

"That makes our primary role as teachers one of helping the kids plan and prepare for the day, rather than in supervising the day itself."

"And that would go a long way towards our objectives of making everything that happens in the new building contribute to the kids' creativity, oral communication, teamwork, and initiative."

"But how would we allocate the building for a whole day? All our timetabling is driven by 40-minute teaching periods."

"Yes, that's true today, but why should that constrain everything? It would be quite unrealistic to expect the kids to carry out something as complex as this in just 40 minutes. Why don't we blow up the rule "the timetable is king," and just timetable the new building differently?"

"But which department would the new building come under?"

"Maybe that's another rule we should blow up. Yes, today we have the biology rooms, the math rooms, the modern languages rooms – petty fiefdoms we all jealously protect. So why don't we make the new building a resource for the whole school, so that the building as a whole, and all the space within it, isn't "owned" by any one department? Wouldn't that really encourage inter-disciplinary working and learning?"

"You know, you've given me an idea. What stops us from blowing up the rules about timetables and ownership even in our existing buildings? Yes, it will be great to have a new building to do all sorts of whizzy new things in, but if we want to create an innovative teaching environment, maybe some of the ideas we've just discussed could apply right now ..."

Key learning

This case demonstrates the power of unlearning. "There is a teacher" is one of the most fundamental aspects of school life, and also one of the most cherished. If you are a teacher, to imagine a world in which teachers do not exist is most uncomfortable. But, as this case study so clearly shows, this is a tremendous springboard to all sorts of ideas, including the shift of emphasis from the teacher-as-the-imparter-of-knowledge-at-the-front-of-the-class to the teacher-as-guide-to-how-the-pupils-can-learn-on-their-own. Powerful stuff indeed.

NESTLÉ UK – WHAT IF WE DIDN'T EAT CHOCOLATE?

One of the most exhilarating workshops I have been involved in was with a division of the world's largest food company, Nestlé: the unit that manufactures and markets the UK's most popular confectionery brand, KitKat, as well as other leaders such as Smarties, After Eights and Aero. Much of the workshop was spent on developing ideas for new brands, but unfortunately I can't talk about these here for they are all confidential. What I can talk about, though, is a discussion resulting from a real raindrop-shaker. One of the assumptions about chocolate is, of course, that "we eat it," so, in the spirit of "How might this be different?," we asked "What if we didn't eat it? What else might we do with it?"

To help this, the group compiled a list of bullet points detailing the features of chocolate, other than that luscious taste, which included:

» Chocolate is fragrant.
» Chocolate is rich in energy.
» Chocolate melts at around 35°C, close to body temperature.
» The melting point depends on the mix of ingredients.
» Chocolate can absorb water from its surroundings.
» Chocolate is a "non-Newtonian fluid" (!) in that it does not flow like other fluids such as water.
» Solid chocolate is quite strong.
» Chocolate is easy to mould.

If chocolate isn't used for eating, its use would need to derive from these other properties, for example:

Fragrance: chocolate could be used as the basis for perfumed soaps, shampoos, air fresheners, scented paper, or in candles.

Energy: could chocolate be used as an energy source, such as a fuel for burning, or perhaps instead of gas in automobiles?

Melting: if chocolate turns from a solid to a liquid at a specific temperature, could it be used in safety devices such as fire sprinklers or fire alarms? Also, if chocolate melts, and then re-solidifies, it often shows a white "bloom," thus showing that melting has taken place. Could this be used as a quality indicator? For example, suppose there is a large shipment of chocolate, associated with, say, five "special" bars which melt at different temperatures. If, on arrival at the destination, all of these are solid, but two have the white "bloom," this would indicate that the shipment had been exposed to a particular temperature.

Water absorbtion: how about using chocolate as an active ingredient in skin creams and face packs?

Special fluid properties: one of these is that, when solid chocolate is subject to a sharp blow, it can extrude through small holes. This suggests that chocolate could act as a shock absorber. Imagine, for example, that there was a solid lump of chocolate behind the bumpers of an automobile. On impact, the chocolate would absorb the shock, and extrude through appropriately designed apertures.

Strength: use chocolate as a construction material in cold climates! For example, at Jukkasjärvi in Swedish Lapland, there is a hotel completely made from ice, which melts every May. So why not build one made of chocolate?

Easy to mould: this suggests using chocolate as a mould for other materials – this would work well since chocolate can form a very precise shape.

Well, I'm sure we'll all continue to eat a lot of KitKats, so it's most unlikely that Nestlé will ever need to invoke these ideas – but it's amazing what ideas a group can come up with in the right environment, once they have gotten comfortable with getting the raindrops out of the valleys!

Key learning

This is a lovely example of what happens when we change our perspective.

> "What do you do with chocolate?"
> "Eat it, of course! What else would you do with it?"

Well, as this case shows, lots of things, potentially.

The case shows the power of listing all the features of the focus of attention, many of which are rarely associated with its primary use. But by listing and examining these features, all sorts of new ideas emerge.

PEARSON TELEVISION – TELEVISION GAME SHOWS

Pearson Television is one of the world's largest producers of television game shows, including programmes such as *The Price is Right*, *Sale of the Century* and *Greed*. Game shows are formulated around very clearly defined formats, which makes it very easy to define the features as required for Step 2 of the ***InnovAction!*** process: these are just a very few of the features, as usual, in no particular order, for *The Price is Right*:

» Contestants are chosen live.
» Contestants are pre-screened.
» The host is enthusiastic.

» Anyone can play.
» The audience guesses too.
» The host doesn't know the prices.
» There is a "Showcase" game.
» Contestants guess prices.
» The audience helps the contestants.
» The contestants can see the goods.
» Contestants are dressed smart-casual.
» Contestants are individuals.
» The show lasts a half hour.
» Prizes are always different.
» The winner is the closest to the right price, without going over.
» The host makes the contestants feel comfortable and safe.
» Contestants can hear and see the studio audience's reactions.
» The TV viewers can see the prizes.
» The key motivation is something for nothing.
» The star prize is worth many thousands of pounds.
» The game does not require literacy.

When the Pearson TV team asked "How might this be different?," this led to all sorts of intriguing places, for example:

» What if contestants were not individuals?
» What if the focus were on a feature other than price?
» What if the price has to be quoted in a different currency?
» What if contestants were not in the studio?
» What if TV viewers could not see the prizes?
» What if contestants were given a week to answer?
» What if there were no host?
» What if the contestant could not hear the audience?
» What if the item you had to guess about were not goods or services?
» What if the host behaved badly?

At the time these lists were compiled, one of these was just becoming evident: the central feature of the BBC's top game show *The Weakest Link* is the singularly aggressive behavior of the UK host, Anne Robinson. Another was implemented a few months later: on New Year's Day 2001 in the UK, the contestants on *Who Wants to be a Millionaire?*

were husband-and-wife couples, rather than individuals – both partners had to agree on the answer!

There's still lots of scope though – the concept of a contestant who cannot hear the audience leads to the "soundproof box," enticing the studio audience to engage in even more bizarre antics to offer advice; the idea of viewers not being able to see the prize leads to the possibility of a game where the audience can't see the prize, but might have other clues to guess the price, or to the thought that the contestant doesn't see the prize, but may perhaps be given an unusual view of part of it, or perhaps a silhouette, and so has to guess what the object is as well as its price.

If the contestants aren't in the studio, then the event could take place on location, leading to cross-overs with programmes such as *Antiques Roadshow*, or a reality game show – what would happen if it took place, for example, on the forecourt of a second-hand car dealer?

And what about the idea that the focus is on something other than price? What might that be? How old an antique is; how big a jewel is; how heavy a casket, full of bank-notes, is. And what about taking the concept of guessing a feature (as in *The Price is Right*), and combining this with the prize from *Blind Date*? What would happen if the objects on *The Price is Right* were not consumer goods, but good-looking members of the opposite sex? What features would you have to guess right to win the prize?

Key learning

This case study shows the power of ***InnovAction!***, especially as applied to processes.

Television game shows all follow a specific formula, and are great examples of Koestler's Law: every game show is a bundled pattern of specific individual components. By teasing out the component parts in terms of the list of bullet points, this provides a wealth of material for asking "How might this be different?," from which ideas flow and flow.

Key Concepts and Thinkers

This chapter presents a glossary of terms from **analogy** (a technique for idea generation) to **unlearning organization** (an organization that has made innovation a way of life).

Cross-references are indicated by the use of ***bold italic***. Numbers in brackets refer to page references in the main text.

analogy – A ***retro-fit*** technique for ***idea generation*** (page 9) in which the key question is "What does [the ***focus of attention***] have in common with [something else]?" For example, asking "What does a restaurant have in common with a theater?" would trigger ideas concerning entertainment, design and ambience. Very similar to ***metaphor*** and ***simile***.

BBC – brain bank connectivity (page 34) – The creativity-enhancing effect attributable to the connectedness between individuals.

blockbuster (page 11) – An idea which, once implemented, achieves great success. Blockbusters are not necessarily ***radical***.

brainstorming (page 20) – An ***idea generation*** technique that starts with a blank sheet of paper, and allows for free thinking in a safe environment. In my view, the use of the blank sheet of paper, which is a symbol of being unconstrained, is in fact counterproductive. ***Innovation*** in business never takes place on a green-field site: rather, it takes place in the context of much learning, knowledge, experience and success. The sheet of paper is not blank – it is very full indeed. Hence the power of ***InnovAction!***.

business concept innovation (page 22) – A concept advocated by Gary Hamel in his book *Leading the Revolution*, in which an organization's entire business model and strategy is radically changed.

Buzan, Tony – The originator of the mind map – a pictorial representation of trains of thought – as portrayed in *The Mind Map Book: Radiant Thinking*, published in 1995.

Christiansen, James A – Author of *Competitive Innovation Management: Techniques to improve innovation performance* and *Building the Innovative Organization: Management systems that encourage innovation*, two books, both published in 2000, which describe the key cultural features of innovative organizations.

creativity (page 9) – The capability to discover new ideas. There is a widely held belief that creativity is an innate gift, with which the fortunate few are born, whilst the rest of us wallow in an uncreative swamp. I do not believe this. In my view, creativity is a skill that can be learnt, practised and enhanced. And as with all human abilities, some people will enjoy doing it more than others, some people will wish to spend more time doing it than others, and some people will be more effective at it than others. But it is an activity to which we can all contribute, and from which no one is excluded. Creativity is not the same thing as *innovation*: creativity is about generating new ideas; innovation is about generating new ideas *and* making something happen as a result.

culture – Organizational cultures have an enormous impact on whether or not it is "safe" to generate new ideas, and how any ideas are evaluated, developed and implemented. This is a really big topic, and covered in its own right in the ExpressExec title *Creating an Innovative Culture*.

de Bono, Edward – Undoubtedly one of the leading thinkers, and certainly the most powerful evangelist, in the field of *creativity* and *innovation*. He is the originator of *lateral thinking*, and the author of a host of books, the best of which (to my mind) is *Serious Creativity*.

de Geus, Arie – A life-long employee of Royal-Dutch Shell who shot to fame with his book *The Living Organization*, which draws a parallel between organizations and living beings. This is an important cultural concept, and has much relevance as regards fostering an innovative culture.

development (page 11) – The stage of the overall *innovation* process in which an idea is made fully fit-for-purpose. See also *Innovation Target*.

evaluation (page 9) – The process by which ideas are judged as "good" or "bad," with the "bad" ones being rejected, and the "good" ones accepted for further exploration, *development* and *implementation*. Evaluation is very important as regards the overall management of the entire *innovation* process (see *Innovation Target*), for it acts as a filter; it is also significant culturally. See also *premature evaluation*.

focus of attention (page 48) – The central theme for *idea generation*, or the definition of the "problem to be solved." When using *InnovAction!*, a relatively narrow focus of attention ("What new restaurant formats can we invent?") is more productive than a broader one ("What new leisure concepts can we invent?").

Gundling, Ernest - Author of *The 3M Way to Innovation*, published in 2000, which is the first book since 1955 to present an in-depth insight into 3M, the company that many would regard as *the* role model for an innovative organization.

Hamel, Gary (page 22) - Leading business guru, with a highly original and provocative style, who passionately believes in the power, and strategic importance, of *innovation*, as expressed in his latest book *Leading the Revolution*.

Hammer, Michael - The originator of the term *business process re-engineering*, and co-author, with James Champy, of the much-quoted article in the July - August 1990 issues of Harvard Business Review, *Reengineering Work: Don't Automate - Obliterate*.

Hebb, Donald (page 44) - The Canadian physiologist who first propounded the theory that learning is a process of organizing the *neurons* in our brains in the form of circuits that are built as a result of experience, and which can then be re-invoked to repeat learned behaviors. This is the basis of the *landscape metaphor for learning*.

How might this be different? (page 49) - The central question in the *InnovAction!* process, which takes a feature of the *focus of attention* as we know it today, and encourages you to explore how that might be different, thus facilitating *unlearning* and creating the conditions for the discovery of new ideas.

idea generation (page 9) - The central process of *innovation*, in which new ideas are created deliberately and systematically. Since innovation in business never occurs on a green-field site, the key skill required is that of *unlearning*. All the tools and techniques to support creativity and idea generation are vehicles to help you unlearn, and they largely fall into two categories: *springboards* and *retro-fits*. See also *Innovation Target* and *InnovAction!*

implementation (page 13) - The final stage of *innovation*, in which an idea comes to full fruition. See also *Innovation Target*.

incremental ideas - Ideas whose features are only modestly changed, as compared to their antecedents or predecessors. Many incremental ideas have turned out to be *blockbusters*. See also *radical ideas*.

InnovAction! (page 48) - A powerful technique for *idea generation* that takes as its starting point a list of features of the *focus of* *attention* as it currently exists. By asking "*How might this be different?*", you are actively encouraged to discover new ideas. Unlike *brainstorming*, which starts from a blank sheet of paper, and *lateral thinking*, which seems to conjure *provocative operations* out of thin air, *InnovAction!* recognizes that the *focus of attention* is likely to be associated with considerable learning, knowledge, and experience, which *InnovAction!* actively uses as a *springboard* to new ideas.

innovation (page 6) - The active management of the four stage process of *idea generation*, *evaluation*, *development* and *implementation*, as applied to the domains of *new product development*, *process innovation*, *organizational innovation*, *relationship innovation*, *strategy* and *you*.

Innovation Target (page 7) - A diagrammatic representation of the four stages of *innovation* (*idea generation*, *evaluation*, *development* and *implementation*) as an archery target, on which are superposed the six domains where innovation can take place (*new product development*, *process innovation*, *organizational innovation*, *relationship innovation*, *strategy* and *you*).

innovative organizations (page 32) - Organizations which have created, built, and sustained an internal capability to make *innovation*, in all its richness, an integral part of their operations. Such organizations are able to solve problems, grasp opportunities, and create their own futures again and again and again and again.

Koestler, Arthur (page 21) - Scholar, soldier and author of many books, including *The Act of Creation*, in which is to be found *Koestler's Law*.

Koestler's Law (page 21) - To my mind, the most powerful definition of creativity:

> "The creative act is not an act of creation in the sense of the Old Testament. It does not create something out of nothing; it uncovers, selects, reshuffles, combines, synthesizes already existing facts, ideas, faculties, skills. The more familiar the parts, the more striking the new whole."

landscape metaphor for learning (page 45) - A metaphor which compares the internal structure of our brains to a richly carved landscape of mountains and valleys. The process of *learning* is portrayed as the creation of the valleys by the action of rain and rivers, so that, once we have learnt something, we are swept down the appropriate valley, and can execute the appropriate actions and behaviors with ease – for example, getting dressed, crossing the road, or driving a car. These activities, of course, are not contentious; but the same also applies to more sophisticated activities, such as managing staff, or formulating strategy. Within this metaphor, *innovation* is a process of escaping from the valley of familiarity, in which a "raindrop" is scooped out of the bottom of a valley, placed on a neighboring ridge, and allowed to remain in this unstable state until it falls into a new valley, the valley of innovation.

lateral thinking (page 20) – A technique of *idea generation* developed by *Edward de Bono*, based on the concept of the "*provocative operation*," which de Bono calls "po." A provocative operation is a deliberate shock to the way we usually see things, and is used as a mechanism to jolt our thinking into new ideas. Two well-known examples of this are "po: planes land upside down" and "po: a factory is downstream of itself."

learning (page 44) – A process in which experience becomes consolidated so that certain behaviors can be repeated, or knowledge recalled, at will. It is now well established that during learning, *neurons* in our brains become "hard-wired," thereby creating semi-permanent neural circuits that store memories, or control learned behaviors. Frequent recall of the memory, or repetition of an action, strengthens these circuits; lack of use allows them to break down, this being an explanation of forgetting. See also *landscape metaphor for learning* and *Donald Hebb*.

learning organization – An organization which has institutionalized a spirit of *learning*.

metaphor – A *retro-fit* technique for *idea generation* (page 9) in which the key question is "How can [the *focus of attention*] be [something else]?" For example, asking "How can a restaurant be a theater?" would trigger ideas concerning entertainment, design and ambience. Very similar to *analogy* and *simile*.

neuron – Cell in the nervous system. *Learning* is a process in which semi-permanent connections are made among specific neurons, so forming a neural circuit which can be activated at will to recall a memory or repeat a learned behavior.

new product development (page 14) – One of the domains where *innovation* is important. See also *Innovation Target*.

nucleotide bases (page 42) – The generic term for the four types of chemical molecule which are string together along DNA, and thereby form genes. The myriad of different sequences of the nucleotides account for the differences between all living things, these patterns being a dramatic example of *Koestler's Law*.

organizational innovation (page 29) – One of the domains where *innovation* is important. See also *Innovation Target*.

Osborne, Alex (page 20) – The American advertising executive who invented *brainstorming*.

premature evaluation (page 100) – A condition, often exhibited by aggressive males, who, in a fit of over-excitement evaluate ideas far too soon, thereby killing innovation stone dead, and creating a most unsatisfying situation for everybody! See also *evaluation*.

process innovation (pages 6 and 28) – One of the domains where *innovation* is important, and sometimes portrayed as business process re-engineering. See also *Innovation Target*.

product innovation (page 8) – One of the domains where *innovation* is important. See also *Innovation Target*.

provocative operation ("po") (page 62) – A deliberate shock to the way we usually see things, and the central feature of *lateral thinking*, used as a mechanism to jolt our thinking into new ideas. Two well-known examples of this are "po: planes land upside down" and "po: a factory is downstream of itself."

radical ideas – Ideas whose features are significantly different from their antecedents or predecessors. Many people believe that only radical ideas can be *blockbusters*, but this is rarely the case – many radical ideas are just too different to be well accepted. See also *incremental ideas.*

raindrop in the valley metaphor for learning (page 45) – See *landscape metaphor for learning.*

random word (page 48) – A *retro-fit* technique for *idea generation* in which a genuinely random word is used as the basis for word association to generate a list of, say, 30 words. These are then used as triggers to see if any ideas arise in connection with any chosen *focus of attention*.

relationship innovation (page 29) – One of the domains where *innovation* is important, applying to the development of new forms of relationship, both within an organization and across the organization's external boundaries. See also *Innovation Target*.

retro-fits (page 57) – A set of techniques for *idea generation* in which your mind is deliberately projected to a place very distant from the chosen *focus of attention*. From this distant standpoint, you are then encouraged to try to discover some connections back to the *focus of attention*, thus discovering new ideas. Examples of retro-fit techniques are *analogy*, *metaphor*, *random word* and *simile*.

Senge, Peter – Author of the business best-seller *The Fifth Discipline*, and advocate of systems thinking and the *learning organization*.

silver bullet (page 2) – Something specific that brings enormous value to your business, such as a *blockbuster* product, a unique business process, or a global brand.

silver bullet machine (page 2) – The organizational capability to produce *silver bullets* again and again and again, so conferring on the organization the ultimate competitive advantage.

simile – A *retro-fit* technique for *idea generation* in which the key question is "How is [the *focus of attention*] like [something else]?" For example, asking "How is a restaurant like a theater?" would trigger ideas concerning entertainment, design, and ambience. Very similar to *analogy* and *metaphor*.

Six Thinking Hats (page 88) – A technique established by *Edward de Bono*, and posited by him as a technique for *idea generation*. My personal view is that the technique is much more powerful when used as a method for *evaluation* rather than *idea generation*.

springboards (page 47) – A set of techniques for *idea generation* which take as the starting point the knowledge, learning, and experience you have of the *focus of attention* as it is now. This detailed information is then used as a springboard for generating new ideas by asking the question "*How might this be different?*" The main technique here is my own *InnovAction!*

strategy innovation (page 14) - One of the domains where *innovation* is important, applying to the development of new business strategies. See also *Innovation Target*.

unlearning (page 46) - The process by which your knowledge, *learning* and experience of a chosen *focus of attention* are decomposed into their component parts. This is a necessary part of the creative process, for this then releases the basic components which can then be reformed into new patterns, in accordance with *Koestler's Law*. Most people find this very difficult – not least because much of our success is attributable to our knowledge, learning, and experience, and the process of disaggregating, decomposing, and challenging these is often most uncomfortable. It is, however, the key to *creativity*. Unlearning must never be portrayed as an attack on the past, or as critical, blame-apportioning, or destructive: rather, it is a constructive process which is a necessary step towards building an innovative future.

unlearning organization - An organization which has institutionalized the processes of *unlearning*, and in which unlearning is not regarded as a threat. Such organizations therefore have built a fundamental capability for discovering new ideas, and so are in a position to capture ultimate competitive advantage.

Resources

This chapter refers you to 27 key books and 18 useful Websites.

There is a lot of good material on innovation, and here is my personal choice.

BOOKS

Allan, Dave, Kingdon, Matt, Murrin, Kris and Rudkin, Daz (1999) *?What if! How to Start a Creative Revolution at Work*. Capstone, Oxford – A lively discussion of "?What if!"'s view on innovation: I particularly enjoyed the chapter on making ideas real.

Christensen, Clayton M. (1997) *The Innovator's Dilemma – When New Technologies Cause Great Firms to Fail*. Harvard Business School Press, Boston, MA – Winner of the Financial Times – Booz Allen and Hamilton 'Best Business Book of 1997' Award, this book lucidly tells how organizations can do many things right, but still end up failing: total customer focus, for example (a "good thing") can blind a company to things customers aren't asking for, or to look for new markets. What these companies fail to do is to manage what Christensen calls "disruptive innovation", and his book tells you how to avoid falling into this trap.

Christiansen, James A. (2000) *Competitive Innovation Management: Techniques to improve innovation performance*. Macmillan Business, Basingstoke, UK.

Christiansen, James A. (2000) *Building the Innovative Organization: Management systems that encourage innovation*. Macmillan Business, Basingstoke, UK – These two books are a matching pair, being based on Christiansen's PhD thesis at INSEAD which studied twenty organizations, eight in depth (including 3M and Eastman Chemical), to discover what made some organizations highly innovative, and others less so. Very thorough, and highly informative.

de Bono, Edward (1993) *Serious Creativity*. HarperCollins, London – A compendium of de Bono's work over the last 25 years. De Bono is a prolific writer: some of his works that are of particular interest are:

de Bono, Edward (1972) *Children Solve Problems*. Penguin Books, Harmondsworth, UK – A wonderfully illustrated collection of how children aged between 5 and 14 solve problems such as "How to stop a dog and a cat from fighting," "How to weigh an elephant" and "How to design a bicycle for mailmen." A powerful exposition of "the learning trap!"

de Bono, Edward (1972) *Po – Beyond Yes and No*. Simon and Schuster, New York, NY – A series of thought-provoking essays.

de Bono, Edward (1986) *Six Thinking Hats*. Viking, London – An exposition of de Bono's process for evaluating ideas safely, using the metaphor of wearing colored hats to legitimize the key roles.

de Bono, Edward (1990) *I Am Right – You Are Wrong*. Viking, London – An impassioned plea for constructive and co-operative exploration and debate, rather than destructive and adversarial advocacy.

de Bono, Edward (1987) *Letters to Thinkers*. George Harrap, London – A series of thought-provoking essays.

de Geus, Arie (1997) *The Living Company: Growth, learning and longevity in business*. Nicholas Brealey Publishing, London–A powerful rallying call to those who believe in the importance of the human spirit in organizations – even large ones. The central metaphor is the organization as a living being.

Foster, Timothy R.V. (1991) *101 Ways to Generate Great Ideas*. Kogan Page, London – An easy-to-read compendium of tools and techniques, structured around 101 brief sections.

Gundling, Ernest (2000) *The 3M Way to Innovation: Balancing people and profit*. Kodansha International, New York, NY – 3M is widely regarded as *the* role model of the innovative organization, and although 3M is widely reported in case studies, this is the first full-length book on 3M to be published since 1955.

Hamel, Gary (2000) *Leading the Revolution*. Harvard Business School Press, Boston, MA – An upbeat, provocative, challenging, and often witty view on strategy, with innovation as the key theme throughout.

Hebb, Donald O. (1949) *The Organization of Behaviour: A neuropsychological theory*. John Wiley & Sons, Chichester, UK – A book in which Hebb explores his hypothesis that the process of learning is one in which neural connections are formed and progressively strengthened.

Jay, Ros (2000) *The Ultimate Book of Business Creativity*. Capstone, Oxford – A thorough description of 36 different creativity techniques, presented as algorithms, rather than with a framework.

Koestler, Arthur (1964) *The Act of Creation*. Hutchinson & Co., London – A book of genius in which polymath Koestler delves into the nature of creativity by exploring the bases of humor, art, and science. Many of the seminal ideas – for example those concerning patterns and the need to unlearn – are discussed most lucidly. There is a health warning, though: this is a book on philosophy rather than management, and more suited to reading on a flight to Australia, rather than a commuter train journey.

Leifer, Richard and McDermott, Christopher M. (2001) *Radical Innovation: How mature companies can outsmart upstarts.* Harvard Business School Press, Boston, MA – This book covers similar territory to Christensen, being based on field-work at companies such as General Motors, General Electric, du Pont and IBM.

von Oech, Roger (1992) *A Whack on the Side of the Head.* Creative Think, Menlo Park, CA – A lively canter through a range of tools and techniques, accompanied by the wisdom of the Creative Whack Pack.

von Oech, Roger (1992) *Creative Whack Pack.* Creative Think, Menlo Park, CA – A pack of 64 "playing cards," each bearing an insightful message concerning creativity and innovation. Also available in disc format for use on personal computers.

Osborn, Alex F, (1993) *Applied Imagination: Principles and procedures of creative problem-solving.* The Creative Education Foundation, Buffalo, New York, NY, 3rd revised edition – One of the creativity classics, by the originator of brainstorming. Contains much good stuff.

Schrage, Michael (2000) *Serious Play: How the world's best companies simulate to innovate.* Harvard Business School Press, Boston, MA – This book stresses the importance of making new ideas as real as possible.

Senge, Peter (1990) *The Fifth Discipline.* Doubleday, New York, NY – A persuasive and articulate exposition of the role of systems thinking in management, alongside the four other key disciplines of "personal mastery," "mental models," "shared vision," and "team learning."

Senge, Peter, Roberts, Charlotte, Ross, Richard, Smith, Bryan and Kleiner, Art (1994) *The Fifth Discipline Fieldbook: Strategies and tools for building a learning organization.* Nicholas Brealey Publishing, London – A companion to *The Fifth Discipline,* packed full of examples, explanations, discussions and anecdotes.

Senge, Peter, Kleiner, Art, Roberts, Charlotte, Ross, Richard, Roth, George and Smith, Bryan (1999) *The Dance of Change: The challenges of sustaining momentum in learning organizations*. Currency Doubleday, New York, NY – An extension of the *Fieldbook*, with yet more examples, explanations, discussions and anecdotes! These two books are, to my mind, amongst the most interesting and informative management texts on the market today.

Sherwood, Dennis (2001) *Smart Things to Know about Innovation and Creativity*. Capstone, Oxford – My most recent book on innovation, packed with examples and case studies, and with a full explanation not only of *InnovAction!*, but of the cultural requirements for building a truly innovative organization too.

Sherwood, Dennis (1998) *Unlock Your Mind: A guide to deliberate and systematic innovation*. Gower Publishing, Aldershot, Hampshire, UK – My earlier book on innovation, with quite a lot on systems thinking too.

VanGundy, Arthur (1988) *Techniques of Structured Problem Solving*. Second edition, Van Nostrand Reinhold, New York, NY – A veritable treasure trove of over 250 tools and techniques!

WEBSITES

If you type "innovation" or "creativity" into a search engine, don't be surprised if you get literally hundreds of thousands of hits. Here are just a very few of them:

www.brint.com

A site specializing in process innovation and business process re-engineering.

www.buffalostate.edu/centres/creativity

The home page of the Center for Studies in Creativity, the research institute set up by Alex Osborne, the inventor of brainstorming. www.buffalostate.edu/~creatcnt/links.html is the address of their links page, which is both comprehensive and independent.

www.cbi.cgey.com

The home page for the Center for Business Innovation of consultants Ernst & Young (now part of the CAP-Gemini empire).

www.cordis.lu/innovation/
The home page of the European Commission's INNOVATION program.

www.csfi.fsnet.co.uk
The site for the Centre for the Study of Financial Innovation, specializing in innovation in finance and financial services.

www.cul.co.uk
The home page of Creativity Unleashed Limited.

www.edwdebono.com
Edward de Bono's official Website.

www.entovation.com
The home page for Entovation International Ltd. an organization specializing in knowledge innovation.

www.expertson.com
A US site covering all aspects of innovation, with many links.

www.ideafinder.com
A wealth of information, with lots of ideas, old and new.

www.ig.com
A site specializing in innovation in local government.

www.jps.net/triz/triz0000
A site all about the Russian TRIZ technique for creativity.

www.mckinsey.com
The home page of the most prestigious consulting firm, McKinsey & Co. Their journal, *The McKinsey Quarterly*, is always worth browsing.

www.redherring.com
The home page for *Red Herring* magazine, whose strapline is *The business of innovation*.

www.silverbulletmachine.com

My own Website!

www.strategos.com

The home page of Gary Hamel's consulting firm, Strategos.

www.thinksmart.com

The home page of the Innovation Network, who, among many other things, offer an Innovation University.

www.trizconsulting.com

The home page for a firm that specializes in the Russian TRIZ technique for creativity.

Ten Steps to Making Innovation Work

This chapter gives you just that – ten key ideas to help you reach the goal of building an organization that really can achieve ultimate competitive advantage.

INNOVATION IS MORE THAN JUST GENERATING IDEAS

Chapters 6 and 7 focused very much on idea generation, the central zone of the Innovation Target. Idea generation is the heart of innovation, and I trust that these chapters have shown how you can do this deliberately, systematically, and safely.

However, as the Innovation Target makes clear, idea generation is only the first stage of a four-stage process – to make something happen, ideas need to be evaluated, so that the best ones can be selected for development and implementation.

From an organizational point of view, "making innovation happen" is all about culture, and I develop this theme in detail in the ExpressExec title *Creating an Innovative Culture*. For completeness, however, let me take this opportunity to outline some of the key points as "ten steps to making innovation work."

1. Make time – and money – available for innovation

Innovation takes time. And we all know how busy we all are – especially after the last decade or so of downsizing. In my experience, the day job is the biggest enemy of innovation. It is so easy for the pressures of the day job to push innovation out of the way. And how many times have I heard "Sorry, we can't do that – it isn't in the budget?"

What do you need time and money for? The answer is:

» *Training* – As I trust Chapters 6 and 7 have made clear, creativity is a skill that can be learnt. But we don't learn it at school, at college or in our professional training. So we need to learn it within our organizations. And that takes some time, and a little money.
» *Idea generation* – This is best done by small, trained groups: in my experience, the ideal size for an idea generation workshop is between 16 and 24 people, working (once they are trained) very intensively for about three hours. Ideally, the groups are diverse, and what better opportunity is there for getting together people who don't normally work with each other? Remember the *BBC*? This too takes some time, and of course some money as well.
» *Evaluation* – I discussed evaluation briefly in Chapter 2, and more thoroughly in *Creating an Innovative Culture*; what is important

here is that this activity also requires time: time to filter the ideas, and time to assess the really good ideas. This can often require a feasibility study of several months' duration, leading to a full business case.

» *Development and implementation* – These can be very time consuming and costly!

» *Knowledge transfer and communication* – These are important components of the infrastructure required to support innovation. They also require active and attentive management, for they do not happen by themselves.

» *Managing the pipeline of ideas* – Truly innovative organizations maintain a continuous flow of ideas. This requires a modest amount of administration, so that ideas don't get lost, and to ensure that the flow of ideas across the four stages of the Innovation Target is well-managed.

Innovative organizations recognize that all these activities directly require time and money, and are pleased to devote the appropriate resources. Why? Because they know that innovation is the source of ultimate competitive advantage. And that it won't happen by itself.

2. Always be searching for better ways of doing things

There is a saying "If it ain't broke, don't fix it" – meaning that you should not interfere with things that are working well. Many organizations take this to an extreme: "We don't fix things until they are broken." Unfortunately, by the time things are broken, it may be too late to fix them, especially in today's fast-changing, hyper-competitive business climate.

Innovative organizations don't wait until things are broken to fix them: they are always searching for new – and better – ways of doing things.

This is not a question of meddling, or changing things just for the sake of changing them. It is a much more constructive, positive process: innovative organizations have a spirit of enquiry; they are constantly aware of what is happening in the outside world; they are not arrogant. The only test of the "status quo" is fitness-for-purpose: if the way things are now continues to be truly fit-for-purpose, then fine, let it be. But if it isn't, it should be changed.

3. Distinguish negligence from learning

Innovation is inevitably risky. By definition, you are doing something new, and that inevitably means that something might not turn out as you intended, or might go wrong. In many organizations, anything that turns out differently from expectations, or that goes wrong, is immediately branded "failure."

No-one likes to fail. So, most people naturally seek to avoid failure. And if the organizational culture is such that everything that is not perfect is by definition a failure, then everyone will seek perfection. As a consequence, they will avoid risk; they will play safe. They will only take those actions that they know will give the "right" result, and, by definition, those actions are necessarily things they have done before. These organizations can therefore never innovate. It's just impossible. No individual will take the risk, and so the organization as a whole is doomed to repeat the mistakes it has made in the past.

From a commercial point of view, this might be successful, at least for a time: if you happen to operate in a market, or in a context, which is changing very slowly, or one which is very protected from competition, then repeating the past might work well. But few of us now, and even fewer of us in the future, will be able to live in such cozy surroundings – and we certainly won't be able to survive.

Innovative organizations have solved the problem of "failure." And one powerful way of doing this is to distinguish "negligence" from "learning."

Negligence is the wilful, or stupid, disregard of organizational rules that are there for a purpose – perhaps concerning health and safety, perhaps concerning financial control. Learning arises when something happens that is different from expectations, and the individuals concerned learn from the experience, and are willing to adapt their behaviors accordingly. Wise organizations punish negligence, but reward learning. And as a consequence, good managers can take the risks associated with innovation without fear.

4. Listen

Listen to other people. Listen to the outside world. Listen to your customers. And your suppliers. And attend to what you hear.

Arrogance is a fundamental block to innovation, and history – business history as well as "real" history – is full of examples of people in positions of authority and power who would not listen to wise advice.

Arrogance is of course the most extreme case of the "learning trap" I discussed in Chapter 6. Arrogant people are so deep within their valleys that they don't even notice where they are, and they certainly don't recognize that there might be any possible other valleys. If you "want to get out of the box" (or the valley!), you first have to acknowledge that the "box" is there. And that's what arrogant people never do.

5. Say "yes" not "no"

Go to a meeting. Take a blank sheet of paper. Draw a line vertically down the center of the paper, and label the left-hand column "yes" and the right-hand column "no." Quietly, and without having anyone else notice, whenever you hear the word "yes," or a corresponding positive remark, put a tick in the left-hand column; put a tick in the right-hand column whenever you hear the word "no" or a corresponding remark. At the end of the meeting, count the number of ticks in each column.

This is a very simple diagnostic of your culture. Macho, adversarial Darwinian cultures have a lot of ticks in the right-hand column. Innovative cultures have more ticks in the left-hand column.

Now, I am not arguing for a "soft" culture in which every goes around hugging each other and any trees that happen to be around. Innovative cultures are not "soft" – in fact they are very disciplined and business oriented. But they have learnt a very important lesson. And that lesson is that ideas can never come to fruition if the idea is never stated in the first place.

And one of the major reasons why ideas do not get stated in uninnovative environments is because people are too scared to do so. Scared that others will laugh, will put the idea down, will say "no." One of the things that junior people learn very quickly in any organization is when it is safe to open their mouths. And if people are scared to open their mouths, the fantastic ideas in their brains are wasted.

6. Don't rush to judge

This is all about premature evaluation – the tendency to rush to judge. One of the most important features of a new idea is that it is not born with a business case, a full cost justification, all the answers. It is very easy to kill a brand new idea – the idea is not well-formulated, I don't know what revenue will be associated with it, and I know there are lots of problems to solve to make the idea work. But I haven't had time to solve all the problems yet. Give me time. Give me time.

Wise organizations recognize this, and allow time for ideas to be explored before passing judgment.

They know, of course, that a judgment must be made, for no organization has the resources to back all ideas, nor would any sensible organization wish to, for inevitably, some ideas really aren't very good. But you can't tell a good idea from a bad one right away: it needs some work, and a wise process.

I describe a wise process in some detail in the accompanying title *Creating an Innovative Culture*: in summary, the process, which is derived from Edward de Bono's *Six Thinking Hats*, is based on examining an idea in a balanced way by asking these questions:

» What are the benefits of the idea?
» What issues need to be managed to make the idea a success?
» How will people feel about the idea?
» What data do we need to be in a position to take a wise and balanced decision?

The first question identifies all the ways in which the idea can bring benefit – such as by revenue enhancement, cost reduction, improved efficiency, better customer relations, or whatever. The second recognizes that, however good the idea, there are inevitably problems to solve, issues to be overcome. This question therefore articulates what these issues are, and identifies ways in which they might be resolved. The third question – concerning how people will feel – is rarely asked in most organizations, but recognizes that many changes are blocked because some people feel aggrieved, damaged, hurt, or just don't like it. This third question addresses these matters directly, thus putting you in a position to be able to manage the change process wisely. And the last question, about data, ensures that all the numbers are there too.

By addressing these questions professionally for any idea, it is then possible to take a balanced judgment. Do the benefits outweigh the problems and costs? How can we assess, and then manage, the risks? Should we proceed with the idea, or shelve it?

At the end of the day, a judgment must be made. But a judgment based on these principles is far, far wiser than one made prematurely, or by advocacy, or by power-play.

7. Get your performance measures right

In my experience, people behave in accordance with their performance measures. That's what they're for, and that's what people do. So if innovation and creativity play no part in people's performance measures, don't be surprised if they fail to be innovative, to come up with new ideas, or to encourage the ideas of others.

8. Ensure that projects can sit safely alongside the line

"Did you hear about Pat?"
"No, I don't think so. What's going on?"
"He's been assigned to a ''special'' project."
"Well, he's on his way out then."

Making innovation happen requires an organizational ability to form, and then disband, project teams. If being assigned to a ''special project'' is regarded as an organizational death warrant, or if anyone who moves out of the line is fearful that there will not be a safe way to return, then projects will either not get started, or – arguably even worse – will get staffed by those whom the organization wishes to fire. In this case, the projects will inevitably fail, thereby discouraging anyone from participating in the next project.

In organizations that make innovation happen, being assigned to a ''special project'' is a sign of organizational favor, and the road to promotion.

9. Embed innovation in the day job

Innovative organizations do not regard innovation as something that only happens at special off-site workshops, or in that department somewhere in marketing. In innovative organizations, innovation is part of the day job. It's embedded in the quality program. In the early stages of the design of a new IT system, the analysts use the ***InnovAction!*** process to ask "How might this be different?" for each element of the process map of the current system. Meanwhile, the directors are using the techniques of deliberate and systematic innovation to determine the scenarios they use as a backdrop to their strategic planning. Yes, innovation really is the natural "way we do things around here."

10. Have the will to do it

Innovation, and building an innovative organization, will not happen by themselves. They will happen only if the organization deliberately makes them happen. And that takes time, money, determination, guts, leadership. Why bother? Isn't it easier to follow the others; to be a "me too" organization; not to rock the boat?

Well, it may be easier. But it sure isn't going to win the prizes of success. As Gary Hamel says, somewhat dramatically, in *Leading the Revolution*:

> "Face it: out there in some garage, an entrepreneur is forging a bullet with your company's name on it. Once the bullet leaves the barrel, you won't be able to dodge it. You've got one option: you have to shoot first. You have to out-innovate the innovators, out-entrepreneur the entrepreneurs. Sound impossible for a decades-old incumbent? It is. Unless you're willing to challenge just about every assumption you have about how to drive innovation and wealth creation in your company."

Innovative organizations are willing to take the time, spend the money, show the determination, bust the guts, demonstrate the leadership to become innovative because they have a belief. A deeply held belief that transcends business cases, cost-benefit analyses and net present values. A belief about their organizational capability to solve problems; to have new ideas again and again and again and again, in whatever domain a new idea might add value; to be truly innovative. A belief that this capability confers the ultimate competitive advantage.

THE TEN STEPS TO MAKING INNOVATION WORK

1. Make time – and money – available for innovation
2. Always keep searching for better ways of doing things
3. Distinguish negligence from learning
4. Listen
5. Say "yes" not "no"
6. Don't rush to judge
7. Get your performance measures right
8. Ensure that projects can sit safely alongside the line
9. Embed innovation in the day job
10. Have the will to do it

Frequently Asked Questions (FAQs)

Q1: What's the difference between creativity and innovation?

A: See Chapter 2.

Q2: Creativity is an inherent gift, isn't it?

A: See Chapter 2.

Q3: We have plenty of ideas, but our problem is making something actually happen. How do we fix that?

A: See Chapter 10.

Q4: Am I right in thinking that innovation is only about the design of new products?

A: See Chapter 2.

**Q5: In my organisation, lots of people have great ideas, and we can cover pages of flip-charts with huge numbers of them. How do we make sense of all this, and how do we select the very best ideas for implementation?

A: See Chapter 2.

Q6: My boss just doesn't understand what it takes to create an innovative environment. What could I suggest she should read to give her some good insights?

A: See Chapter 5.

Q7: From a commercial point of view, innovation is inherently risky. Aren't we better off not being innovative, but just copying other people's ideas?

A: See Chapter 2.

Q8: I've heard the term *lateral thinking* – but what exactly is it?

A: See Chapters 3 and 6.

Q9: Where can I find a good checklist we can use to assess how good (or bad!) we are at innovation?

A: See Chapter 2.

Q10: Where can I find a good checklist we can use to help our organisation to become more innovative?

A: See Chapter 10.

About the Author

Dennis Sherwood originally trained as a research scientist, and was for twelve years an IT consulting partner with Deloitte, Haskins & Sells, and, following the merger in the UK, Coopers & Lybrand. He was then appointed an Executive Director with Goldman Sachs in London, and is now the Managing Director of *The Silver Bullet Machine Manufacturing Company Limited*, which specializes in organizational creativity and innovation. Dennis is well-known on the conference circuit, and is the author of five books, including *Smart Things to Know about Innovation and Creativity*, published by Capstone in 2001.

Index